THE   BOOK   OF

REGIONAL AMERICAN COOKING
SOUTHWEST

JAN NIX

Photographed by
GLENN CORMIER

HPBooks
a division of
PRICE STERN SLOAN
Los Angeles

ANOTHER BEST-SELLING VOLUME FROM HPBooks

HPBooks
a division of Price Stern Sloan, Inc.
11150 Olympic Boulevard
Los Angeles, California 90064
© 1993 Price Stern Sloan, Inc.

By arrangement with Salamander Books Ltd.

10 9 8 7 6 5 4 3 2 1

Photography by Glenn Cormier
Food Stylist: David Pogul
Assistant Food Stylist: Alba Cera

Library of Congress Cataloging-in-Publication Data

Nix, Janeth Johnson.
    The book of regional American cooking. Southwest / Jan Nix : photographed by Glenn Cormier.
        p.   cm.
    Includes index.
    ISBN 1-55788-074-3
    1. Cookery, American—Southwestern style. I. Title.
TX715.2.S69N59 1993
    641.5979—dc20   93-2088
                                                                        CIP

Printed in Hong Kong

Special thanks for props to: Penny Lakes, Bo Danica, La Jolla; Anne Hakes, Williams-Sonoma, San Diego; Bill Demert, The Pottery Shack, Laguna Beach; Susan Bass, Old Town Pottery, San Diego; and Gayle Kellner, Bazaar del Mundo, San Diego.

CONTENTS

A M E R I C A N

INTRODUCTION

The zesty cuisine of the American Southwest—New Mexico, Arizona and Texas—evolved from a rainbow of cultures, and this book contains recipes from each. The original landholders were Native Americans, followed by Spaniards and Mexicans. Each offered agricultural crops and time-honored dishes which, through time, were blended to forge a new cuisine. Later, the cowboy, pioneer and settler broadened the cooking base. The result is a kaleidoscope of dishes that are mouthwatering, full flavored and festive.

Beyond taste, Southwestern cuisine has bold visual appeal: from brick-red dried chiles to slate-blue cornmeal, from pale brown, pinto-spotted and black beans to vivid green tomatillos, avocados and cacti. Texture adds another exciting dimension: from the rough blistered surfaces of tortillas to the chunky consistency of salsas to the velvety smoothness of cheese melting into red chile sauce.

Though steeped in tradition, contemporary Southwest cooking continues to grow and evolve. In the hands of innovative chefs and home cooks, age-old ingredients are given a new twist, a more stylish presentation, in some cases a cross-cultural blending with touches from Asia or France. Expanded marketing of produce has infused year-round freshness to a cuisine originally shaped by the seasons.

Whether you prefer to cook by tradition or chart a new course within traditional boundaries, you'll find recipes here, old and new, to bring the full spectrum of tantalizing Southwestern tastes to your own table.

Ingredients

For the most part, the recipes in this book call upon everyday ingredients found in well-stocked supermarkets. The placement of items is not the same in all markets: canned and dry goods may be shelved in the Mexican or ethnic food section, while unusual produce is generally displayed alongside the more familiar fruits and vegetables. For a wider selection, you may wish to visit your nearest Mexican market.

CHILES

From mild to wild, chiles are a staple in nearly every Southwestern meal. While dozens of varieties are grown and their uses overlap, the chiles used in this book are limited to those readily available. A note of caution: Be careful not to touch your eyes after handling chiles and thoroughly wash any skin area that comes into contact with chile's volatile oils, concentrated especially in the interior veins. If your skin is sensitive, you may want to wear rubber or plastic gloves when handling chiles.

Dried Chiles

Because they're always available, dried chiles are more important in Southwestern cuisine than fresh ones. Look for cellophane bags of whole dried red New Mexico or California chiles or the darker broad ancho (sometimes called pasilla) chiles in Mexican grocery stores or the Mexican products section or fresh produce section of well-stocked markets. Dried chiles are toasted briefly, simmered or soaked in hot water and pureed in a blender before using. These chiles are also sold ground in small cellophane bags for recipes which call for ground red chile. To make your own ground chile, toast the dried chiles on a baking sheet in a 350F (175C) oven for 5 to 10 minutes or until very dry and crisp. When chiles are cool, discard stems and seeds, crumble dried chiles into an electric spice grinder and process into powder. If a few seeds are still visible, strain through a sieve. One dried red chile makes roughly 1 tablespoon ground red chile.

Green Chiles

These large mild green chiles are widely available canned, either whole or diced. Or you can buy fresh Anaheim, also called California green chiles, or the broader, slightly more spicy poblano chiles and prepare them for cooking in one of several ways. First cut a small slit near the stem end of each chile. If you have a gas range, roast the chiles, one at a time, over the flame, until they are blistered and lightly charred. For a large quantity, you can roast chiles on the barbecue over low glowing coals. Or place chiles in a shallow-rimmed pan, 2 inches below a preheated broiler, and broil, turning frequently, until lightly charred. After roasting chiles by any technique, place them in a plastic bag while still warm; seal. Let chiles sweat until cool enough to handle, then peel off the skins. If chiles are going to be chopped or pureed, discard the stem, seeds and veins. If you want to keep the chiles whole for stuffing, make a slit down one side and snip out the seed pocket and veins with scissors. Use chiles, refrigerate for up to 3 days or freeze.

Other Chiles

To give food a fiery bite, you can use the small (2- to 3-inch) jalapeño chiles and serrano chiles interchangeably. Although available canned or pickled, they are generally used fresh with the stems, seeds and membranes removed to make them less hot. And how hot is hot? Generally smaller chiles pack the biggest punch, but there's no sure way to predict how hot any fresh chile will be. Climate and soil influence the level of heat and it's possible that 2 chiles harvested from the same plant will produce 2 different levels of fire. The surest way is to taste a sliver before adding the amount recommended in each recipe. If you prefer more heat, mince the chiles without removing the seeds.

Chipotle is not a variety of chile, but a dried jalapeño with a smoky flavor. Sometimes sold as whole dried chipotle chiles, they are more typically sold canned en escabeche (a pickling mixture) or in adobo (a tomato-base sauce).

OTHER INGREDIENTS

Achiote Seeds (annatto seeds)

Earthy in flavor, these tiny rusty-red seeds are used primarily for color. To use as a powder, grind seeds in a spice grinder and use like paprika to coat meats. To color oil, heat 2 parts vegetable oil and 1 part seeds over low heat until the oil is bright orange; discard seeds and use oil as you would any fat in cooking.

Almonds

These are the preferred nuts in Spanish-inspired sauces and desserts.

Anise Seeds

These seeds are used to give a licorice taste to sweet pastries, particularly the holiday cookies, biscochiotos.

Avocado

For richest flavor and most buttery texture, look for California-grown avocados: the oval-shaped, bumpy-skinned Haas or the pear-shaped, smooth-skinned Fuerte.

Blue Cornmeal

Made from native New Mexican blue corn, this has a slightly more bitter taste than yellow or white cornmeal and a distinctive slate-blue color. Look for blue cornmeal in supermarkets in boxes or in bulk bins or in health food stores.

Cajeta

This Mexican-style ready-to-use caramel sauce comes in several flavor variations. The original style is a simple combination of goat milk, sugar, vanilla and cinnamon. Sold in jars, it can be stored indefinitely in the refrigerator after opening.

Chayote

This pale-green pear-shaped squash with deeply furrowed skin was grown centuries ago by the Aztecs and Mayas of Mexico. To prepare it, wash well, then slice through the seed, which is edible.

Chili Powder

This is the blend of ground spices commonly associated with the Texas-style "bowl of red." Unlike ground red chile which is made only from dried chiles, chili powder is flavored with cumin and oregano. For Southwestern dishes, most cooks prefer to start with pure ground chile and add other seasonings to taste.

Chorizo

This refers here to Mexican chorizo, a highly seasoned, coarsely ground pork sausage sold in links of various sizes. To cook, remove the casing, crumble the meat into a pan and fry slowly using low heat so the spices do not burn. The supermarket selection of this sausage varies in flavor and quality. For a mild-flavored, lower-fat chorizo, make your own sausage patties (page 52).

Cilantro

Also called Chinese parsley or fresh coriander, this fresh herb has a distinctive pungent flavor. For cooking, chop the leaves and tender stem tips with a chef's knife. For garnishing, use whole sprigs. To store, wash well, dry in a lettuce spin-dryer, place in a plastic bag and refrigerate.

Cooking Fats & Oils

The preferred fat for many traditional Southwestern dishes is lard, but home cooks and chefs today are bending tradition to focus on lighter flavor and health. In keeping with this shift, the recipes in this book call for vegetable oil, olive oil, butter and vegetable shortening.

Coriander Seeds

Sold as whole seeds or ground, these are the seeds of the cilantro or coriander plant. Coriander seeds have a warmer, less pungent flavor than cilantro leaves and cannot be substituted for the fresh herb.

Cumin

Sold as whole seeds or ground, cumin has a warm, slightly bitter flavor which enlivens almost any chile-based sauce, but particularly the red.

Jicama

This Mexican root vegetable looks like a giant-size brown-skinned turnip. With its white flesh, crisp texture and slightly sweet flavor, it is delicious raw or cooked. To use, remove peel, then slice or chop.

Juniper Berries

These dried blue berries give gin its distinctive flavor. In Southwestern cooking, Pueblo Indian cooks add them to stews and game dishes for a bittersweet accent. Look for them in supermarket spice shelves.

Masa Harina

This is dehydrated corn flour that is used to make masa, the dough from which tortillas and tamales are made.

Nopales

These big round pads of the prickly pear cactus are sometimes sold fresh, but are more commonly found canned in jars. They offer a crisp texture and flavor something like pickled green beans.

Oregano

Also called wild marjoram, this aromatic herb is available fresh, dried or ground. It has a pleasant bitter undertone that especially complements dried chiles and tomatoes.

Pecans

Large pecan orchards dot the Southwest, where pecans are used extensively in appetizers through desserts.

Piloncillo

This dark-brown Mexican raw sugar with a molasseslike taste comes in hard cones of varying sizes. To use, shred on a grater or shave off the desired amount with a knife.

Pine Nuts

As demand outstrips supply, native piñon nuts, which ripen in pine cones throughout Southwest desert areas, are hard to find and expensive. Imported pine nuts make a good substitute.

Pumpkin Seeds

Also called pepitas, these dark-green shelled pumpkin seeds are sold roasted and raw. Store in the refrigerator or freeze. Like nuts, they turn rancid if held too long at a warm room temperature.

Tomatillos

These look like large green cherry tomatoes enclosed in papery husks. Sold fresh and canned, their mildly acidic flavor provides the base for many Southwestern salads and salsas. Tomatillos can be eaten both raw and cooked: Simply remove the husks and wash the sticky-skinned fruit before using.

Tortillas

Corn tortillas have withstood the test of time, but variations on the basic flour tortilla are offered in a dizzying array. Besides the traditional white flour tortilla, you can choose whole wheat, sprouted wheat, lard based and oil based. Sizes range from a thicker 6- to 7-inch fajita style to a thinner 12-inch burrito style.

To heat corn or flour tortillas, place in a dry skillet over medium heat and cook, turning once or twice, until soft and pliable. Keep hot in an insulated tortilla warmer until ready to serve. To heat in an oven, moisten tortillas with wet hands, stack and seal in foil. Heat in a 325F (165C) oven for 10 to 12 minutes. To heat in a microwave oven, stack moistened tortillas on a paper towel and put into a plastic bag; loosely close. Cook in a microwave oven on HIGH power until hot, 30 to 60 seconds depending on the number of tortillas.

SALSA FRESCA

4 medium-size tomatoes
2 fresh jalapeño or serrano chiles
1/2 cup chopped green onions and tops
1/4 cup chopped white onion
1/4 cup chopped cilantro
2-1/2 tablespoons fresh lime juice
1/4 teaspoon salt
1/8 teaspoon pepper
Lime wedges for garnish

Core tomatoes and cut in half; squeeze each half gently to force out seeds. Coarsely chop tomatoes and place into a bowl.

Cut off chile stems; quarter each chile lengthwise. With the tip of a sharp knife, cut off and discard seeds and membranes. Cut each chile into julienne strips; stack strips and cut crosswise to finely mince.

In a medium-size bowl, combine tomatoes, chiles, green onions, white onion, cilantro, lime juice, salt and pepper. Cover and refrigerate at least 1 hour for flavors to blend or up to 3 days.

Makes 3 cups.

Variation
Cut 1/2 avocado into 1/4-inch pieces. Fold into salsa and chill.

JALAPEÑO SALSA

8 fresh jalapeño or serrano chiles
1 tablespoon vegetable oil
1/4 cup chopped onion
1 garlic clove, minced
1 can (about 1-lb.) tomatoes, undrained
1 tablespoon red wine vinegar
1 tablespoon chopped cilantro
1/4 teaspoon salt

Cut off chile stems. Quarter chiles lengthwise and remove seeds. Cut each piece in half or thirds. Process chiles in a food processor until finely chopped.

Heat oil in a 2-quart pan over medium heat. Add onion, cover and cook until onion is soft but not brown, 4 to 5 minutes. Add chiles and garlic; cook, uncovered, 2 minutes.

Finely chop tomatoes; add tomatoes and their liquid to pan. Simmer, uncovered, 10 minutes. Add wine vinegar. Simmer 5 more minutes. Remove from heat and add cilantro and salt. Let salsa stand until cool. Serve at once or cover and refrigerate up to 1 week.

Makes 1-1/2 cups.

TOMATILLO SALSA

1/2 pound tomatillos
2 teaspoons chipotle chiles en escabeche
1/4 cup finely chopped onion
2 tablespoons chopped cilantro
1 tablespoon fresh lime juice
1/4 teaspoon salt

Remove papery husks from tomatillos; wash tomatillos. Without removing cores, cut the tomatillos into slices 1/4 inch thick.

Stack slices, a few at a time, and cut into strips 1/4 inch wide. Cut across strips to make 1/4-inch cubes.

Measure 2 teaspoons of chiles including sauce. Place on cutting board and finely chop. In a medium-size bowl, combine tomatillos, chiles, onion, cilantro, lime juice and salt. Cover and refrigerate 1 hour or up to 3 days to allow the flavors to blend.

Makes 2 cups.

GUACAMOLE

2 large avocados
2 tablespoons finely chopped red onion
1 fresh jalapeño or serrano chile, seeded
    and minced
2 tablespoons chopped cilantro
2 tablespoons fresh lime juice
1/4 teaspoon salt
Pepper
Onion rings and cilantro leaves for garnish

Cut avocados in half lengthwise around pit. Holding each half, twist to remove one side from pit. Thrust a knife into pit and twist to remove.

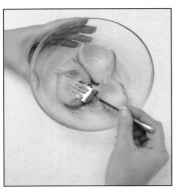

With a salad fork, scoop avocado flesh into a medium-size bowl; coarsely mash with fork.

Stir in onion, chile, cilantro and lime juice; mix well. Add salt to taste, starting with 1/4 teaspoon. Add pepper to taste. Serve, or cover and refrigerate up to 2 hours.

Makes 2 cups.

Variation
To serve as a salad, spoon over shredded lettuce and garnish with tomato wedges.

BLACK BEAN DIP

2 cups drained cooked black beans (Frijoles, page 76)
About 1/2 cup black bean cooking liquid
1-1/2 tablespoons vegetable oil
1 small onion, finely chopped
1 fresh jalapeño or serrano chile, seeded and minced
2 garlic cloves, minced
4 ounces goat cheese (chevre)
1 cup (4 oz.) shredded Monterey Jack cheese
Hot pepper sauce
Salt
1 small green onion (including top), thinly sliced
Tortilla chips

In a food processor, process beans with 1/4 cup of bean liquid until smooth; reserve remaining bean liquid. Heat oil in a 2-quart saucepan over medium heat. Add onion; cover and cook until onion is soft but not brown, 4 to 5 minutes. Add chile and garlic; cook 1 minute. Stir in beans. Cook over low heat until beans are hot.

Crumble in goat cheese, reserving about 1 tablespoon for garnish; add Monterey Jack cheese. Cook, stirring occasionally, until cheeses are melted. Add hot pepper sauce and salt to taste. Transfer to a heatproof serving dish or fondue pot; keep warm over heat source. If dip becomes too thick, stir in 1 or 2 tablespoons of reserved bean liquid. Garnish with the reserved goat cheese and green onion. Serve with tortilla chips.

Makes about 8 servings (2-1/2 cups).

CHILE CON QUESO

Vegetable oil for deep-frying
6 corn tortillas, cut into wedges
3 fresh jalapeño or serrano chiles
1 tablespoon vegetable oil
1 small onion, chopped
1 large tomato, chopped
1/4 cup half and half
8 ounces pasteurized processed cheese
    spread, cut into chunks
1/2 cup (2 oz.) shredded Monterey
    Jack cheese
1/2 cup (2 oz.) shredded Cheddar cheese

Pour oil into a deep 2-quart pan to a depth of 1 inch and heat to 360F (180C). Fry tortilla pieces, a few at a time, until crisp and lightly browned, 1 to 2 minutes. Remove with a slotted spoon; drain on paper towels.

Seed and mince 2 of the chiles; cut remaining chile crosswise into thin slices. Heat oil in a 2-quart pan over medium heat. Add onion; cover and cook until onion is soft but not brown, 4 to 5 minutes. Add tomato and all chiles; cook, uncovered, until tomato is soft, 4 to 5 minutes.

Add half and half; cook over low heat until bubbly. Add processed cheese; stirring, cook until it melts. Add remaining cheeses and stir until mixture is evenly blended. Pour into a fondue pot or place over a warmer. Serve with tortilla chips.

Makes about 6 servings (2 cups).

Nachos Rancheros

3/4 cup (3 oz.) shredded Cheddar cheese
3/4 cup (3 oz.) shredded Monterey
  Jack cheese
6 cups corn tortilla chips
2 chipotle chiles en escabeche, thinly sliced
About 1/3 cup each guacamole, dairy sour
  cream and salsa

In a bowl, combine cheeses. Place 1/3 of tortilla chips in an ovenproof dish 9 to 10 inches in diameter and about 1-1/2 inches deep, such as a quiche dish.

Sprinkle with 1/3 of the chiles and 1/3 of the cheese. Repeat 2 more times so chips resemble a round haystack.

Just before serving, preheat oven to 325F (165C). Bake nachos just until cheese melts, 5 to 6 minutes. Spoon guacamole, sour cream and salsa in separate mounds on top of nachos. To eat, pick up a chip and scoop out condiments as desired.

Makes 4 servings.

Variation
Cook 4 ounces chorizo sausage until crumbly and well browned; drain on paper towels. Sprinkle chorizo over tortilla chips as you layer the nachos.

SHRIMP QUESADILLA

4 teaspoons butter or margarine
4 (about 8-inch) flour tortillas
1 cup small cooked shrimp, patted dry
1/4 cup diced green chiles
1 cup (4 oz.) shredded Cheddar cheese
Sunflower sprouts for garnish

Green Chile Dip:
1/2 cup dairy sour cream
1 green onion (including top), sliced
1/4 cup diced green chiles
2 tablespoons chopped parsley
2 tablespoons chopped cilantro
1/4 teaspoon dried leaf oregano
1/8 teaspoon garlic salt

To prepare Green Chile Dip: Process all ingredients in a food processor until smooth. Cover and refrigerate 1 hour.

For each quesadilla, melt 1 teaspoon of the butter in a wide skillet with a non-stick finish over medium heat. Place 1 tortilla in pan; when tortilla is slightly warm, place 1/4 cup of the shrimp, 1 tablespoon of the green chiles and 1/4 cup of the cheese on half of tortilla.

Fold tortilla over cheese to make a half circle. Cook, turning as needed, until cheese is melted and tortilla is lightly browned on both sides, 2 to 3 minutes. Remove from pan and keep warm. Repeat with remaining tortillas, adding 1 teaspoon butter to pan for each quesadilla. Cut quesadillas into pie-shaped wedges. Serve with chile dip. Garnish with sunflower sprouts.

Makes 4 servings.

BLUE CORNMEAL QUESADILLAS

1 large egg
3/4 cup milk
1/3 cup all-purpose flour
1/3 cup blue cornmeal
1 teaspoon vegetable oil
Dash of salt
7 teaspoons butter or margarine
4 green onions (including tops), thinly sliced
6 ounces goat cheese (chevre), crumbled
Tomatillo Salsa (page 15)

Prepare **crepes:** In a blender or food processor, process egg and milk until blended. Add flour, cornmeal, oil and salt; process until smooth.

Melt 1/4 teaspoon butter in a 7- to 8-inch skillet with a nonstick finish over medium-high heat. Stir batter; pour 3 tablespoons into pan. Tilt pan to coat evenly. Cook crepe until top side is dry and underside is lightly browned. Turn and cook other side about 10 seconds. Slide out of pan onto paper towel. Repeat, buttering pan and stirring batter before making each crepe. For quesadillas, melt 1 teaspoon of the butter in a wide skillet; add onions and cook 1 minute. Remove from skillet; wipe pan clean with a paper towel.

Melt 1 teaspoon of the butter in skillet. Cover half of each crepe with 1/8 of green onion and 1/8 of cheese; fold crepes in half to make half circles. Cook quesadillas, turning as needed, until cheese is softened and crepes are lightly browned, 1 to 2 minutes. Keep warm. Cut into wedges and serve with salsa.

Makes 8 crepes, 8 servings.

– Scallop & Shrimp Seviche –

1/2 pound sea scallops
1/3 cup fresh lime juice
2 tablespoons each olive oil, fresh orange
   juice and chopped cilantro
1 medium-size tomato, diced
1/4 cup finely chopped red onion
3 to 4 teaspoons minced fresh jalapeño or
   serrano chile
1/2 pound small cooked shrimp, patted dry
1/4 teaspoon salt
Lettuce leaves
1 avocado
1 lime

Cut scallops crosswise into 1/8-inch-thick slices; place in a shallow bowl.

Cover with lime juice; press scallops in an even layer so all slices are submerged in juice. Cover and refrigerate until scallops are opaque, 4 hours or as long as overnight. In a large bowl, combine olive oil, orange juice, cilantro, tomato, onion, chile and shrimp. Drain scallops, reserving 3 tablespoons of the marinade. Add scallops, reserved marinade and salt to bowl; stir gently to mix.

Cover and refrigerate until ready to serve. Arrange lettuce leaves in 6 cocktail glasses. Halve, seed and peel avocado. Cut each half into 6 crescents; cut lime into wedges. Garnish each serving with avocado and lime.

Makes 6 servings (3 cups).

— CHICKEN FILO TRIANGLES —

1 (3-oz.) package cream cheese, softened
1 (4-oz.) can diced green chiles, drained and
   patted dry with paper towels
1 (2-1/4-oz.) can sliced pitted ripe olives,
   drained
1 green onion, finely chopped
1 cup diced cooked chicken
16 sheets filo pastry
3/4 cup butter or margarine, melted
3 tablespoons cornmeal mixed with 1 teaspoon mild ground red chile for topping

In a bowl, combine cream cheese, chiles, olives and onion; mix well. Fold in chicken.

Place 1 filo sheet on a work surface; cover remaining filo with a towel. Brush lightly with melted butter. Top with another sheet of filo and butter. Cut filo crosswise into 5 equal strips each about 2-1/2 inches wide and 12 inches long. Place a rounded teaspoon of filling on one end of each strip. Fold over one corner to make a triangle. Fold the triangle over again on itself. Continue folding, from one side to the other. Trim edge, if needed.

Place triangles on an ungreased baking sheet, brush with butter and sprinkle with seasoned cornmeal. Repeat until all triangles are folded. Cover and refrigerate up to 24 hours or freeze. Bake triangles, uncovered, in a preheated 350F (175C) oven 15 minutes (20 to 25 minutes if frozen), or until golden-brown. Let triangles cool 5 minutes before serving.

Makes 40 appetizers.

— SOUTHWEST SUSHI ROLLS —

1 (8-oz.) package cream cheese, softened
1/4 cup peeled, roasted red bell pepper
   (page 9), patted dry with paper towels
1/2 teaspoon grated lemon peel
1/4 cup loosely packed cilantro
1 avocado
2 teaspoons fresh lime juice
1/8 teaspoon salt
5 (about 10-inch) flour tortillas
1 (3-oz.) pkg. smoked salmon, in strips
4 green onions (including tops), thinly sliced
4 ounces sliced smoked turkey breast
Radishes and sunflower sprouts for garnish

For cheese spread, process cream cheese, bell pepper, lemon peel and cilantro in a food processor until smooth.

Peel and pit avocado. Place in a small bowl and mash coarsely with a fork. Stir in lime juice and salt. Working with 1 tortilla at a time, lightly moisten both sides with water. Spread about 3 tablespoons cheese spread on tortilla. Partially cover lower third of tortilla with 1/3 of salmon strips. Using 1/5 of avocado mixture, make a band across center of tortilla. Sprinkle with onions.

Roll up. Repeat with 2 more tortillas and remaining salmon. Repeat with remaining tortillas and turkey, placing turkey over two-thirds of each tortilla. Wrap each roll in plastic wrap. Refrigerate 2 hours to firm cheese spread or up to 8 hours. To serve, trim 1/2 inch from each end; discard ends. Cut each roll into 8 slices. Garnish with radishes and sprouts.

Makes 40 appetizers: 24 with smoked salmon, 16 with smoked turkey.

CHILE CHEESE PUFFS

1/2 cup water
3 tablespoons butter or margarine
1/8 teaspoon salt
1/2 cup all-purpose flour
2 large eggs
2 teaspoons minced fresh serrano chile
1/3 cup shredded Swiss cheese
1-1/2 tablespoons grated Parmesan cheese

Preheat oven to 400F (205C). Lightly grease a baking sheet. In a 2-quart pan over medium heat, bring water, butter and salt to a boil. When butter melts, add flour all at once and stir vigorously with a wooden spoon until dough forms a ball in center of pan. Remove from heat. Add eggs, one at a time, beating well after each addition until dough is shiny-smooth. Stir in chile and cheeses.

On greased baking sheet, drop about 1-1/2 teaspoons dough for each puff, about 2 inches apart. Bake 15 minutes or until outside is lightly browned and crisp. Remove baking sheet from oven. Without lifting puffs, cut a slit in lower side of each puff with the tip of a sharp knife to let steam escape. Return to oven, turn off heat and let stand 10 minutes.

Cool thoroughly on racks. **Cheese Filling:** In a small bowl, beat 6 ounces softened cream cheese and 3 tablespoons sour cream until smooth; stir in 1/4 cup finely chopped sun-dried tomatoes and 1/4 teaspoon garlic salt. Cut each puff in half; fill each with about 2 teaspoons filling. Replace tops, cover and refrigerate up to 2 hours.

Makes about 24 puffs.

SHRIMP GAZPACHO

1 medium-size cucumber, peeled, seeded, and coarsely chopped
1/2 red bell pepper, coarsely chopped
1/2 green bell pepper, coarsely chopped
1/2 small onion, coarsely chopped
3 medium-size tomatoes
2 cups tomato juice
2 tablespoons chopped cilantro
1 teaspoon minced fresh jalapeño chile
2 tablespoons olive oil
1-1/2 tablespoons red-wine vinegar
2 teaspoons fresh lime juice
1/2 teaspoon salt
4 ounces small cooked shrimp
Cilantro sprigs for garnish

In a food processor, process cucumber, bell peppers and onion until finely chopped. Pour into a large bowl.

Blanch tomatoes in boiling water 30 seconds; place in cold water to cool. Peel off skin, core tomatoes and cut into 1/4-inch pieces. Place tomatoes in bowl with cucumber mixture.

Add tomato juice, chopped cilantro, chile, olive oil, wine vinegar, lime juice, salt and shrimp. Stir until evenly mixed. Cover and refrigerate at least 4 hours. Serve cold in chilled bowls. Garnish with cilantro sprigs.

Makes 6 servings (6 cups).

— Chilled Avocado Bisque —

1 large ripe avocado
About 1 cup regular-strength chicken broth
1/2 cup dairy sour cream
1/2 cup plain yogurt
2 teaspoons fresh lime juice
1/8 teaspoon ground cumin
3 to 5 drops hot pepper sauce
Salt
Minced chives and pear tomatoes, to garnish

Halve and seed avocado. With a tea-spoon, scoop out flesh and drop into food processor bowl or blender.

Process avocado until smooth. Add 1 cup chicken broth, the sour cream, yogurt, lime juice and cumin. Process until smooth. If avocado is very large, add 1 or 2 more spoonfuls of chicken broth and process to make soup the desired consistency.

Pour into a bowl. Add hot pepper sauce and salt to taste. Cover and refrigerate at least 2 hours. Serve cold in small chilled bowls. Garnish each serving with chives and tomatoes.

Makes 4 servings (3 cups).

AZTEC SOUP

Vegetable oil for deep-frying
2 corn tortillas, cut into 1/8-inch strips
2 teaspoons vegetable oil
1/2 cup chopped onion
1/2 cup thinly sliced celery
2 garlic cloves, minced
1 teaspoon minced fresh jalapeño chile
1 (about 1-lb.) can tomatoes, undrained
4 cups regular-strength chicken broth
1 cup frozen whole-kernel corn
1 teaspoon ground cumin
1 cup shredded cooked chicken
1 tablespoon fresh lime juice

Pour 1/2 inch oil into a small skillet over medium-high heat. When oil is hot, add tortilla strips, a few at a time, and deep-fry 1 minute or until crisp and lightly browned. Transfer with a slotted spoon to paper towels to drain.

Heat the 2 teaspoons oil in a 3-quart pan over medium heat. Add onion, celery, garlic and chile. Cover and cook until onion is soft but not brown, 4 to 5 minutes. Coarsely chop tomatoes; add to pan. Add chicken broth, corn and cumin. Bring to a boil. Cover, reduce heat and simmer 10 minutes. Add chicken and lime juice. Simmer 5 minutes. Serve soup in individual bowls. Garnish with tortilla strips.

Makes 4 servings (about 6 cups).

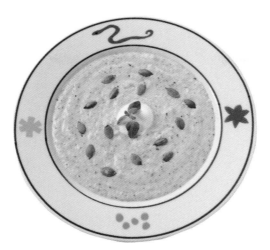

ZUNI SQUASH SOUP

1 tablespoon butter or margarine
1 medium-size onion, cut in half, thinly
   sliced
1 garlic clove, minced
1-1/2 pounds zucchini or crookneck squash
   or a mixture of both, thinly sliced
1/3 cup canned diced green chiles
2 cups regular-strength chicken broth
1 bay leaf
1/2 teaspoon dried leaf oregano
1/8 teaspoon pepper
1/2 cup pumpkin seeds, toasted
1/2 cup dairy sour cream
1/4 teaspoon salt
1/4 cup dairy sour cream and oregano sprigs
   for garnish

Melt butter in a 3-quart pan over medium heat. Add onion and garlic; cover and cook until onion is soft but not brown, 4 to 5 minutes.

Add squash, chiles, chicken broth, bay leaf, oregano and pepper. Bring to a boil. Cover, reduce heat and simmer until squash is tender, 20 to 25 minutes. Remove and discard bay leaf.

In a food processor or blender, puree soup with 1/3 cup of the pumpkin seeds until smooth. (The pureed seeds will still be slightly crunchy.) Return to pan. Whisk in sour cream and salt to taste starting with 1/4 teaspoon. Heat through without boiling. Ladle soup into individual bowls. Garnish with sour cream, oregano sprigs and remaining pumpkin seeds.

Makes 4 servings (4-1/4 cups).

CORN & OYSTER STEW

2 tablespoons butter or margarine
2/3 cup chopped onion
1/2 cup thinly sliced celery
4 ears corn, kernels cut from the cobs and milk scraped out, or 3 cups frozen whole-kernel corn
1 (4-oz.) can diced green chiles
2 cups regular-strength chicken broth
1 bay leaf
1/2 teaspoon ground red chile
2 cups half and half
10 to 12 ounces shucked fresh oysters with their liquor
1 tablespoon each chopped celery leaves and chopped cilantro for garnish
Lemon peel for garnish

Melt butter in a 3-quart pan over medium heat. Add onion and celery, cover and cook until onion is soft but not brown, 4 to 5 minutes. Add corn, green chiles, chicken broth, bay leaf and ground chile. Bring to a boil. Cover, reduce heat and simmer until vegetables are very tender, 20 to 25 minutes. Remove and discard bay leaf.

In a food processor or blender, puree soup. Return soup to pan. Whisk in half and half and cook until soup is hot but not boiling. Cut oysters in bite-size pieces. Add oysters and their liquor; cook until edges of oysters begin to curl, 2 to 3 minutes. Ladle soup into individual bowls. Sprinkle garnish over each serving.

Makes 4 servings (5-1/2 cups).

WILD RICE & CORN CHOWDER

4 ounces chorizo sausages, casings removed
1 small onion, chopped
2 celery stalks, diced
1/2 red bell pepper, diced
1 garlic clove, minced
3/4 cup wild rice, rinsed and drained
3 cups regular-strength chicken broth
1-1/2 cups frozen whole-kernel corn
2 cups half and half
1 teaspoon each dried leaf thyme and basil
1/2 teaspoon ground red chile
Thinly sliced red chiles for garnish

Crumble chorizo into a 5-quart pan. Cook over medium-low heat, stirring occasionally with a fork, until sausage is lightly browned.

Add onion, celery, bell pepper and garlic. Cover and cook over medium heat until onion is soft but not brown, 4 to 5 minutes. Add wild rice and chicken broth. Bring to a boil. Cover, reduce heat and simmer until rice is tender, 40 to 45 minutes. Tilt pan and skim off fat with a large spoon.

Add corn, half and half, thyme, basil and ground chile. Simmer until corn is tender, 5 to 6 minutes. Ladle into individual bowls. Garnish each serving with chile slices.

Makes 4 servings (5-1/2 cups).

Note
When fat is skimmed off, the red color is removed with the fat.

Black Bean Soup

1 pound dried black beans, soaked
 overnight, drained
1 (1-lb.) ham shank
2 medium-size onions, chopped
1 large celery stalk, chopped
1 large carrot, chopped
4 garlic cloves, coarsely chopped
1 (49-1/2-oz.) can regular-strength
 chicken broth
4 cups water
1 tablespoon ground red chile
2 teaspoons ground cumin
1/2 teaspoon pepper
1/4 cup dry sherry
Salt
1/2 cup dairy sour cream mixed with
 2 tablespoons milk for garnish

Place drained beans, ham shank, onions, celery, carrot, garlic, chicken broth and water into an 8-quart kettle.

Bring to a boil. With a large spoon, skim off foam that rises to surface. Add ground chile, cumin and pepper. Cover, reduce heat and simmer until beans are tender, about 2 hours. Remove shank with a slotted spoon; let cool. Cut off meat and return to kettle; discard skin and bone. In a food processor or blender, puree soup a portion at a time; return to kettle.

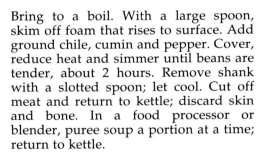

Stir in sherry and salt to taste. Heat to a simmer. Ladle soup into individual bowls. Drizzle sour cream-milk mixture over each serving.

Makes 6 to 8 servings (11-1/4 cups).

TEX-MEX CHILI

8 ounces chorizo sausages, casings removed
1-1/2 pounds beef round steak, cut into 1/2-
inch cubes
1 large onion, chopped
2 garlic cloves, minced
1 to 2 teaspoons minced fresh jalapeño or
serrano chile
2 tablespoons chili powder
1 teaspoon ground cumin
1 (about 1-lb.) can tomatoes, undrained
1 (12-oz.) bottle beer
Lime wedges and parsley for garnish

Crumble chorizo into a 3- to 4-quart pan. Cook over medium-low heat, stirring occasionally with a fork, until sausage is lightly browned and begins to release fat. Add steak and cook over medium-high heat until meat is lightly browned. Add onion, garlic, fresh chile, chili powder, cumin, tomatoes and beer. Bring to a boil.

Skim off fat. Cover, reduce heat and simmer 1-1/2 hours. Simmer with lid ajar 30 more minutes or until steak is very tender and chili has thickened slightly. Ladle chili into individual bowls. Garnish with lime wedges and parsley.

Makes 4 to 6 servings (6 cups).

– Cowboy Chili with Beans –

1-1/2 tablespoons vegetable oil
2 medium-size onions, chopped
3 garlic cloves, minced
2-1/2 pounds beef round, trimmed, cut into
**   1/4-inch cubes or coarsely ground**
3 cups water
1 (28-oz.) can crushed tomatoes with puree
1 (7-3/4-oz.) can Mexican-style tomato sauce
3 tablespoons ground red chile
1 teaspoon ground cumin
1/2 teaspoon dried leaf oregano
4 cups drained cooked pinto beans
1/2 teaspoon salt
Green onions for garnish

Heat oil in a 5-quart pan over medium heat. Add onions and garlic; cover and cook until onions are soft but not brown, 4 to 5 minutes.

Add meat all at once; cook over high heat, stirring frequently, until meat is gray but not browned. Add water, tomatoes, tomato sauce, ground chile, cumin and oregano. Bring to a boil. Cover, reduce heat and simmer until meat is tender, about 1-1/4 hours.

Stir in beans. Simmer, uncovered, 30 minutes or until chili has thickened slightly. Add salt to taste, starting with 1/2 teaspoon. Ladle chili into individual bowls. Garnish with green onions.

Makes 6 to 8 servings (11 cups).

— Chicken & Bean Chili —

1 pound dried Great Northern beans, soaked
 overnight, drained
2 medium-size onions, chopped
5 garlic cloves, minced
1 (49-1/2-oz.) can regular-strength chicken
 broth
1-1/2 to 2 pounds boneless chicken thighs,
 cut into 1-1/2-inch pieces
1/4 teaspoon each salt and pepper
2 tablespoons vegetable oil
2 fresh jalapeño chiles, seeded and minced
1 (7-oz.) can whole green chiles, cut into 3/4-
 inch-wide strips
2 teaspoons ground cumin
1 teaspoon ground coriander
1/2 teaspoon ground cinnamon
1/4 cup chopped cilantro
Sliced pitted ripe olives for garnish

Place drained beans, 1 onion, 2 garlic
cloves and chicken broth in an 8-quart
kettle. Bring to a boil. Cover, reduce heat
and simmer until beans are tender, 1 to
1-1/2 hours. Drain, reserving liquid.

Sprinkle chicken with salt and pepper.
Heat 1 tablespoon of the oil in a 5-quart
pan over medium-high heat. Add chick-
en and cook until lightly browned, 5 to
6 minutes. Remove chicken from pan.

Heat the remaining oil in pan over
medium heat. Add remaining onion,
remaining garlic and fresh chiles. Cook
until onion is soft but not brown, about
5 minutes. Return chicken to pan. Add
green chiles, spices, beans and 2 cups of
the bean liquid. Bring to a boil. Cover,
reduce heat and simmer 30 minutes.
Serve with olives.

Makes 6 to 8 servings (about 10 cups).

Feast Day Posole

1 (2-lb.) lean boneless pork butt, cut into
   4 chunks
2 pounds pork neck bones
4 dried red New Mexico chiles,
   seeds removed
2 medium-size onions, coarsely chopped
4 large garlic cloves, minced
2 teaspoons dried leaf oregano
1 teaspoon cumin seeds
1/2 teaspoon black peppercorns
12 cups water
1 (29-oz.) can hominy, drained
1 teaspoon salt or to taste
8 radishes, shredded or thinly sliced, to serve
1 avocado, sliced, to serve

Bring pork, chiles, onions, garlic, oregano, cumin seeds, peppercorns and water to a boil in an 8-quart kettle.

Cover, reduce heat and simmer 2 hours or until meat is tender. Remove meat with a slotted spoon; let cool. Shred meat; discard fat and bones. Cover and refrigerate until needed. Pour broth through a sieve set over a large bowl; discard solids. Cool broth; cover and refrigerate overnight so fat hardens. Lift off and discard fat.

Reheat broth to a simmer. Add hominy. Cover and simmer 30 minutes. Return meat to broth; heat until hot. Add salt to taste. Ladle posole into individual bowls. Serve with radishes and avocado.

Makes 6 servings (about 12 cups).

Green Chile Stew

2 tablespoons vegetable oil
1 large onion, chopped
3 garlic cloves, minced
1 fresh jalapeño chile, seeded and minced
2 pounds lean boneless pork butt, cut into
   3/4-inch cubes
2 tablespoons tomato paste
1 (about 1-lb.) can tomatoes, undrained
2 (7-oz.) cans whole green chiles, cut into 1-
   inch-wide strips
1 medium-size potato, peeled and grated
2 cups water
1/2 teaspoon each ground cumin and dried
   leaf oregano
1/2 teaspoon salt or to taste

Heat oil in a 5-quart pan over medium heat. Add onion, garlic and fresh chile. Cover and cook until onion is soft but not brown, 4 to 5 minutes. Add pork and cook, uncovered, stirring occasionally, until meat has lost all pink color, about 10 minutes. Stir in tomato paste until evenly blended. Coarsely chop tomatoes; add to pan.

Add green chiles, potato, water, cumin and oregano and bring to a boil. Cover, reduce heat and simmer 1 hour or until meat is tender. Add salt to taste, starting with 1/2 teaspoon. Uncover and simmer 15 minutes or until stew is thickened to your liking. Ladle stew into individual bowls.

Makes 6 servings.

Juniper Lamb Stew

3 tablespoons masa harina
1/2 teaspoon each salt and pepper
2 pounds cubed boneless lean lamb
2 tablespoons vegetable oil
1 large onion, chopped
2 large tomatoes, peeled and chopped
1 green bell pepper, cut into 3/4-inch pieces
1 (15-oz.) can hominy, drained
1/3 cup chopped celery leaves
2 tablespoons ground red chile
2 teaspoons dry juniper berries, crushed
2 (14-1/2-oz.) cans beef broth

Combine masa harina, salt and pepper in a plastic bag. Add meat and shake bag until meat is evenly coated. Heat 1-1/2 tablespoons of the oil in a 5-quart pan over medium-high heat. Add meat, a few pieces at a time, and cook until browned. Remove meat from pan. Heat the remaining 1/2 tablespoon oil in pan over medium heat. Add onion, cover and cook until onion is soft, 4 to 5 minutes.

Return meat to pan. Add tomatoes, bell pepper, hominy, celery leaves, ground chile, juniper berries and broth. Bring to a boil. Cover, reduce heat and simmer 1-1/4 hours or until meat is tender.

To make dumplings: During the last 15 minutes of cooking, combine 1/2 cup each flour and blue cornmeal, 1 teaspoon baking powder and 1/4 teaspoon salt in a medium-size bowl. Cut in 2-1/2 tablespoons butter until mixtures resembles coarse meal. Add 1/2 cup milk and stir with a fork until dough leaves sides of bowl. Drop dough onto stew to make 12 small dumplings. Cover and simmer 18 minutes or until dumplings are firm.

Makes 6 servings.

Huevos Rancheros

2 tablespoons vegetable oil
1 small onion, chopped
1 garlic clove, minced
1 (about 1-lb.) can tomatoes, undrained
1/3 cup each diced roasted green chile and
    roasted red bell pepper
1/2 cup chicken broth
1/4 teaspoon each ground cumin and dried
    leaf oregano
Salt and pepper
4 to 8 corn tortillas
4 to 8 fried eggs
1 (1-lb.) can refried black beans, heated
Avocado slices and cilantro sprigs for garnish

Heat the 2 tablespoons oil in a wide skillet over medium heat. Add onion and garlic and cook until onion is soft, 4 to 5 minutes.

Chop tomatoes; add to pan with green chile, bell pepper, chicken broth, cumin and oregano. Cook, uncovered, over medium heat, until sauce is thickened and reduced to 2 cups, about 10 minutes. Add salt and pepper to taste.

For soft tortillas, heat tortillas in an ungreased skillet over medium-high heat 45 seconds on each side or until soft; keep warm in a covered bowl. For soft-fried tortillas, heat 1/2 inch oil in a small skillet over medium-high heat. Cook tortillas, 1 at a time, until soft, about 10 seconds. Drain on paper towels. For each serving, place 1 or 2 tortillas on a plate, top with 1 or 2 fried eggs and 1/2 cup sauce. Serve refried beans alongside. Garnish as desired.

Makes 4 servings.

BREAKFAST BURRITOS

4 (8-inch) flour tortillas
1 tablespoon each butter and vegetable oil
1/2 small onion, chopped
1 fresh jalapeño chile, seeded and minced
1 (4-oz.) can diced green chiles, drained
2 cups cubed cooked red potatoes (3 large)
Salt and pepper
4 large eggs, lightly beaten
1 cup (4 oz.) shredded Monterey Jack cheese
Salsa Fresca (page 13)

Preheat oven to 325F (165C). Wrap tortillas in foil and place in oven 5 to 10 minutes to warm.

Heat butter and oil in a wide skillet over medium heat. Add onion and fresh chile and cook until onion is soft, 4 to 5 minutes. Add green chiles and potatoes; cook until potatoes are browned. Add salt and pepper to taste. Pour eggs into pan; cook, stirring occasionally, until eggs are set but still creamy. Remove from heat and stir in half of the cheese.

Divide egg mixture among the warmed tortillas; overlap sides or roll to enclose egg mixture. Top each burrito with a spoonful of salsa and a sprinkle of the remaining cheese.

Makes 4 servings.

Variation
Omit jalapeño chile; add 8 ounces Chorizo Sausage Patties (page 52) or chorizo sausage. Cook with onion until sausage is browned and crumbly before adding eggs.

Chile Rellenos

6 large mild green chiles
1/2 pound Monterey Jack cheese
1/2 cup all-purpose flour plus extra
2 large eggs, separated
1/2 cup milk
1/4 teaspoon salt
Vegetable oil for frying
Jalapeño Salsa (page 14), heated

Preheat broiler. Cut a small slit near stem end of each chile. Place in a shallow pan, 2 inches below heat, and broil, turning frequently, until blistered and lightly charred. Immediately place chiles in a paper bag; seal. Let cool. Leave stems on chiles; peel off skins. Carefully slit each chile down one side; snip off seeds and veins with scissors.

Cut cheese into sticks about 1/2 inch wide, 1/2 inch thick and 1 inch shorter than chiles. Stuff cheese sticks into chiles. Dust chiles with flour. In a blender, process egg yolks, milk, the 1/2 cup flour and the salt until smooth. In a small bowl, beat egg whites until stiff; fold into yolk mixture.

Heat 1/4 inch oil in a wide skillet over medium heat. Drop a large spoonful of egg mixture into pan; lay a stuffed chile in middle of egg mixture. Top and enclose chile with another spoonful of egg mixture. Cook 2 minutes or until golden-brown; gently turn and cook 2 or 3 minutes longer or until golden. Keep warm in a 200F (105C) oven. Spoon salsa over each serving.

Makes 6 servings.

GREEN-CHILE FILO PUFF

1 green onion (including top), thinly sliced
3 tablespoons melted butter or margarine
4 sheets filo pastry
2 tablespoons yellow cornmeal
3/4 cup (3 oz.) shredded Cheddar cheese
1/3 cup canned diced green chiles, patted dry
3 large eggs
1 cup milk
1/4 teaspoon salt
1/8 teaspoon white pepper

Preheat oven to 350F (175C). Butter a 1-quart soufflé dish. In a small skillet, cook green onion in 1 teaspoon of the butter 1 minute.

Place 1 filo sheet on a work surface; cover remaining filo to prevent drying. Brush lightly with about 2 teaspoons butter; sprinkle with 1 teaspoon of the cornmeal. Repeat with remaining filo, placing remaining sheets on buttered filo, brushing each sheet lightly with butter and sprinkling with cornmeal. Sprinkle cheese over bottom half of top filo sheet. Sprinkle green onion and chiles over cheese. Very loosely, roll filo jellyroll style. Coil the roll loosely in buttered dish. Brush with remaining butter and sprinkle with remaining cornmeal.

In a medium-size bowl, beat eggs; stir in milk, salt and pepper. Pour into center of dish. Bake, uncovered, until a knife inserted in center of custard comes out clean and filo is puffed and golden-brown, 45 to 50 minutes. Serve immediately.

Makes 4 servings.

TROUT WITH SAGE

1/4 cup shelled pistachios
1/4 cup all-purpose flour
2 tablespoons rubbed sage
1 teaspoon salt
4 whole trout (about 8 oz. each), ready
   to cook
Pepper
3 tablespoons olive oil
Lemon slices and fresh sage for garnish

In a food processor, process nuts with flour until very finely chopped. Pour into a shallow dish; mix in rubbed sage and 3/4 teaspoon of the salt.

Rinse fish in cool water; drain, but do not dry. Sprinkle the remaining 1/4 teaspoon salt and pepper to taste in fish cavities. Dredge each fish in nut mixture until coated on both sides.

Heat 2 tablespoons of the oil in a wide skillet over medium heat; place 2 trout in pan. Cook, turning once, until coating is golden-brown and fish just begins to flake, 4 to 5 minutes on each side. Transfer fish to a platter; cover loosely and keep warm. Repeat with remaining oil and trout. Garnish with lemon slices and fresh sage.

Makes 4 servings.

SWORDFISH WITH CORN SALSA

4 swordfish steaks (1-1/2 lbs.), 1 inch thick
1 garlic clove, cut in half
1 tablespoon each olive oil and lemon juice
Salt and pepper

Corn Salsa:
3/4 cup cooked whole-kernel corn
1 large tomato, cut into 1/4-inch pieces
1/4 cup chopped onion
2 teaspoons minced fresh jalapeño chile
1 tablespoon lemon juice
1 garlic clove, peeled
1 lemon, cut into wedges for garnish

Rub fish with cut garlic; brush with oil and lemon juice. Season with salt and pepper. Let stand 30 minutes.

To prepare salsa: Combine corn, tomato, onion, chile and lemon juice in a small bowl. Stick a wooden pick into peeled garlic; bury in salsa. Let stand 30 minutes for flavors to blend.

Preheat charcoal grill and grease grill rack. Place fish on grill 4 to 6 inches above coals. Cook, turning once, 4 to 5 minutes on each side or until fish turns from translucent to opaque and just begins to flake. Discard garlic clove and serve salsa with fish. Garnish with lemon wedges.

Makes 4 servings.

FISH WITH CHILE CREAM

2 dried ancho (pasilla) chiles, toasted
6 sun-dried tomato halves
2/3 cup whipping cream
3 tablespoons dry white wine
Pinch each ground cumin and dried leaf
   oregano
1-1/2 pounds firm-textured white fish fillets
Salt and pepper
All-purpose flour
1 tablespoon each butter and vegetable oil
2 tablespoons pine nuts
Parsley sprigs for garnish

To prepare chile cream: In a small pan, cook chiles in simmering water 20 minutes; drain. In a small bowl, cover dried tomatoes with 1/2 cup warm water; let stand 15 minutes.

In a blender, process chiles, tomatoes and 1/4 cup of tomato soaking water until pureed. Push puree through a wire strainer; discard residue. Place puree in a small pan; whisk in cream, wine, cumin, oregano and salt. Simmer over low heat until sauce thickens enough to coat a spoon.

Lightly sprinkle fish with salt and pepper. Dust with flour, shaking off excess. Melt butter in a wide skillet over medium heat. Add pine nuts and cook until golden-brown; remove with a slotted spoon and set aside. Add oil to pan. Add fish and cook, turning once, until fish is golden-brown and just begins to flake, 4 to 7 minutes. Serve sauce over fish and sprinkle with pine nuts. Garnish with parsley.

Makes 4 servings.

Spicy Grilled Shrimp

3 tablespoons vegetable oil
2 tablespoons tomato-based chili sauce
1 tablespoon fresh lime juice
1 teaspoon ground mild red chile
1/2 teaspoon salt
2 tablespoons chopped cilantro
1-1/2 pounds large raw shrimp, shelled and
  deveined

Mango Salsa:
1 mango, peeled and cut into 1/4-inch cubes
2 tablespoons diced red bell pepper
1 tablespoon minced red onion
1 tablespoon chopped cilantro
2 teaspoons minced fresh jalapeño chile
1 tablespoon fresh lime juice
Salt

In a medium-size bowl, whisk oil, chili sauce, lime juice, ground chile and salt; stir in cilantro. Add shrimp and mix well. Cover and refrigerate 1 hour.

To prepare salsa: In a bowl, combine mango, bell pepper, onion, cilantro, chile and lime juice; add salt to taste. Cover and refrigerate 1 hour.

Lift shrimp from marinade and drain; reserve marinade. Thread shrimp on skewers. Preheat charcoal grill and grease grill rack. Place skewers 4 to 6 inches above coals. Cook, turning once and basting with reserved marinade, 3 to 4 minutes on each side or until shrimp turn pink. Serve with salsa.

Makes 4 servings.

CRAB ENCHILADAS

4 medium-size tomatoes, chopped
1 small onion, coarsely chopped
1 garlic clove, cut in half
1 (4-oz.) can diced green chiles
Vegetable oil
1/4 teaspoon salt
1/2 pint (1 cup) whipping cream
3/4 pound crabmeat or small cooked shrimp
1/4 cup prepared salsa verde
12 corn tortillas
1 cup (4 oz.) shredded Monterey Jack cheese
1/4 cup grated Parmesan cheese
Jalapeño chile, sliced into rounds for garnish

In a blender or food processor, process tomatoes, onion, garlic and green chiles until pureed. Heat 1 tablespoon oil in a wide skillet; add tomato mixture and salt. Cook over medium heat until sauce is thickened, 8 to 10 minutes. Whisk in 1/2 cup of the cream. Combine crabmeat and salsa in a bowl.

Heat 1/2 inch of oil in a small skillet over medium-high heat. Place 1 tortilla in oil; cook 2 seconds on each side or just until limp. Lift out with tongs, drain briefly, then dip in tomato-cream sauce. Transfer sauced tortilla to a plate. Place 1/4 cup crabmeat across center of tortilla; roll up and place in a baking dish. Repeat with remaining crabmeat and tortillas.

Pour remaining tomato-cream sauce and remaining cream over enchiladas. Preheat oven to 350F (175C). Bake, covered, 20 minutes or until heated through. Sprinkle with cheeses. Bake, uncovered, 10 minutes or until cheeses melt. Garnish with jalapeño rounds.

Makes 6 servings.

–LAMB WITH PINEAPPLE SALSA–

2 tablespoons minced chile chipotle en escabeche
2 garlic cloves, minced
1 tablespoon olive oil
1 teaspoon each ground cumin, dried rosemary and dried leaf oregano
1/2 teaspoon each salt and pepper
1 (4- to 5-lb.) boned and rolled leg of lamb

Pineapple Salsa:
2 cups diced fresh pineapple
1/3 cup chopped red onion
1 fresh jalapeño chile, seeded and minced
3 tablespoons chopped cilantro
2 tablespoons chopped fresh mint
1-1/2 tablespoons fresh lime juice
1 tablespoon honey
1/8 teaspoon salt
Mint sprigs for garnish

Preheat oven to 325F (165C). In a small bowl, combine chile chipotle, garlic, olive oil, cumin, rosemary, oregano, salt and pepper.

Untie lamb and spread open; rub the inside with half of chile mixture. Reform lamb into a compact roll; tie tightly with kitchen string. Rub remaining chile mixture over lamb. Place lamb on a rack in a roasting pan. Roast meat, uncovered, until meat thermometer registers 140F (60C) for rare, 25 to 30 minutes per pound. Let rest 15 minutes before carving. Skim fat from pan drippings; reheat drippings and pass at the table.

While meat is roasting, prepare salsa: Mix all ingredients in a bowl; cover and refrigerate 1 hour. Serve salsa with lamb. Garnish with mint sprigs.

Makes 8 to 10 servings.

– Barbecued Baby Back Ribs –

4 pounds baby back ribs
1/2 onion, sliced
1 garlic clove
1 teaspoon each salt, black peppercorns and
    red pepper flakes
1/4 cup vegetable oil
1/2 cup chopped onion
2 garlic cloves, minced
1 (8-oz.) can tomato sauce
1/2 cup each packed brown sugar, cider vine-
    gar and water
2 tablespoons each Worcestershire sauce,
    molasses and tomato paste
1 teaspoon each ground cumin and chili
    powder
1/2 teaspoon each black pepper and red
    (cayenne) pepper

Simmer ribs in a deep pot with 8 cups water, sliced onion, whole garlic, salt, peppercorns and pepper flakes, covered, 50 minutes; drain.

Heat oil in a 2-quart pan over medium heat. Add onion and garlic, and cook until onion is soft, 4 to 5 minutes. Add tomato sauce, brown sugar, vinegar, water, Worcestershire sauce, molasses, tomato paste, cumin, chili powder, black pepper and cayenne. Simmer, stirring occasionally, 30 minutes or until sauce is reduced to 2-1/4 cups.

Preheat charcoal grill and grease rack. Place ribs 4 to 6 inches above coals and cook until lightly browned, 10 to 15 minutes. Brush sauce over all sides. Grill, brushing frequently with sauce, until ribs are tender and well glazed, 6 to 8 minutes per side.

Makes 6 servings.

Carnitas Salad

1-1/2 pounds boneless pork butt, cut into 1-inch cubes, fat trimmed
1 cup water
1/2 cup apple juice
1-1/2 teaspoons ground mild red chile
1/2 teaspoon each ground cumin, salt and pepper
1 bay leaf
2 tablespoons each olive oil and fresh lime juice
1 teaspoon sugar
1 small red onion, thinly sliced
1 head butter lettuce
1 bunch watercress, tough stems removed
2 oranges, peeled, quartered lengthwise, thinly sliced crosswise
1 cup matchstick jicama pieces
1/4 cup coarsely chopped cilantro

Prepare Carnitas: In a deep skillet, combine meat, water, apple juice, ground chile, cumin, salt, pepper and bay leaf. Bring to a boil; reduce heat, cover and simmer 1 hour or until meat is tender when pierced.

Discard bay leaf. Cook, uncovered, over medium heat until most of liquid evaporates and meat browns slightly, 8 to 10 minutes. Skim and discard fat.

In a small bowl, combine olive oil, lime juice and sugar. Add onion and let stand 30 minutes. Place lettuce leaves, watercress, oranges, jicama and cilantro in a large salad bowl. Add onion mixture and toss. Add salt and pepper to taste. Spoon warm carnitas over salad; toss gently.

Makes 6 to 8 servings.

CARNE ADOVADA

5 or 6 dried red New Mexican chiles
2 dried ancho (pasilla) chiles
2 cups water
1/4 cup fresh orange juice
1/2 teaspoon each ground cumin, dried leaf
   oregano and salt
2 pounds lean boneless pork butt, cut into
   1/2-inch-thick slices
1 medium-size onion, sliced
2 garlic cloves, minced
Flour tortillas, warmed, and Guacamole
   (page 16), to serve

Rinse chiles. In a dry skillet over medium-low heat, toast chiles until they puff slightly and smell toasty, 3 to 4 minutes. Discard stems and seeds. In a medium-size pan, cover and simmer chiles in water 20 minutes.

In a blender or food processor, process chiles with 1-1/2 cups of the water until pureed. Push puree through a wire strainer; discard residue. In a 5-quart non-reactive pan, combine chile puree, orange juice, cumin, oregano and salt. Add meat, onion and garlic; mix well. Cover and refrigerate 1 to 2 days.

Preheat oven to 325F (165C). Bake meat, covered, 2 to 2-1/2 hours or until meat is very tender. Skim and discard fat. Return to oven and bake, uncovered, 20 to 30 minutes or until sauce is consistency of canned tomato sauce. Serve in warm tortillas with Guacamole.

Makes 6 to 8 servings.

— CHORIZO SAUSAGE PATTIES —

2 pounds boneless pork butt, cubed
3 tablespoons water
1-1/2 tablespoons distilled white vinegar
2 tablespoons ground mild red chile
1/2 to 1 teaspoon ground hot red chile
1-1/4 teaspoons salt
1/2 teaspoon ground cumin
1/4 teaspoon each ground coriander and
    dried oregano
2 garlic cloves, minced
1 tablespoon vegetable oil
2 teaspoons achiote seeds (optional)

Spread meat in a shallow pan; freeze 20 to 30 minutes or until firm but not frozen solid. In a food processor, process meat, a portion at a time, until finely chopped but not pasty. Place meat in a large bowl.

In a small bowl, combine water, vinegar, ground chiles, salt, cumin, coriander, oregano and garlic. Add to meat and mix well. Cover and refrigerate at least 24 hours but no longer than 2 days. Divide meat into 8 parts; shape each into a 1/2-inch-thick patty. Cook at once or freeze up to 1 month.

To cook sausage, place oil in a wide skillet. For characteristic red color, add achiote seeds to oil; cook over low heat until seeds turn very dark red and oil is a deep red color. Discard seeds. Add sausage, and cook over medium heat until well browned, about 8 minutes on each side.

Makes 8 patties.

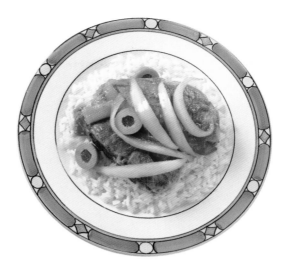

– RANCH-STYLE PORK CHOPS –

2 tablespoons vegetable oil
1 tablespoon chili powder
1/2 teaspoon ground cumin
4 (1-inch-thick) large loin pork chops
1 large onion, thinly sliced lengthwise
2 large garlic cloves, thinly sliced
2 tablespoons dry red wine or water
1 (about 1-lb.) can tomatoes, undrained
1 (4-oz.) can whole green chiles, cut into 1-
  inch pieces
1/4 cup pimento-stuffed green olives, each
  cut in half
Salt
Cooked rice, to serve

In a small bowl, make a paste of 1 table-spoon of the oil, the chili powder and cumin. Spread on both sides of meat.

Heat remaining tablespoon oil in a deep skillet over medium-low heat. Add onion, garlic and wine. Cover and cook until liquid has evaporated and onion is soft and golden-brown, 12 to 15 minutes. Remove from pan. Add meat and cook over medium-low heat until browned on each side, 5 to 6 minutes total. Cut up tomatoes; add to pan with liquid. Add onion mixture, green chiles and olives.

Cover and simmer, turning halfway through cooking, until meat near bone is no longer pink when slashed, 30 to 35 minutes. Remove meat to a platter. Cook sauce, uncovered, over medium-high heat until thickened slightly, 4 to 5 minutes. Add salt to taste. Spoon sauce over meat. Serve with rice.

Makes 4 servings.

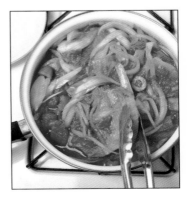

VENISON & CHIPOTLE CREAM

1/2 cup dry red wine
2 tablespoons vegetable oil
1 tablespoon Worcestershire sauce
4 dried juniper berries, crushed
1 garlic clove, minced
1/4 teaspoon each salt and pepper
1 pound venison or beef steaks, cut
   1/2 inch thick
1/4 cup roasted red bell pepper
1 to 2 teaspoons chopped chiles chipotle en
   escabeche
2 tablespoons canned beef broth
1 tablespoon butter or margarine
2 tablespoons minced shallots
1/4 cup whipping cream
Cilantro sprigs for garnish

In a small bowl, combine 1/4 cup of the wine, 1 tablespoon of the oil, the Worcestershire sauce, juniper berries, garlic, salt and pepper. Place meat in a heavy plastic bag, add marinade and seal bag. Refrigerate 8 hours.

In a blender, puree bell pepper, chipotle chiles and broth. Drain meat; pat dry and rub off seasonings with paper towels. Heat the remaining oil in a wide skillet over medium-high heat. Add meat; cook until browned on both sides but still pink in center, 4 to 5 minutes. Transfer to a platter.

Wipe pan clean. Melt butter in pan over low heat. Add shallots; cook 2 minutes. Add the remaining wine; simmer until reduced by half. Stir in chile puree and cream; simmer until sauce is thick enough to coat a spoon, 2 to 3 minutes. Spoon sauce over meat. Garnish with cilantro.

Makes 4 servings.

RABBIT WITH MUSTARD CREAM

1/2 cup all-purpose flour
1 teaspoon each dry mustard and dried
    leaf thyme
1/2 teaspoon each salt and pepper
1 (2-1/2- to 3-lb.) fryer rabbit, cut up
1-1/2 tablespoons each butter and
    vegetable oil
2 tablespoons minced shallot
About 3/4 cup hard cider
1/2 cup whipping cream
1 teaspoon mustard seeds
1 teaspoon grated lemon peel
1-1/2 tablespoons fresh lemon juice
Salt
2 tablespoons chopped parsley

Combine flour, dry mustard, thyme, salt and pepper in a shallow bowl. Pull off and discard lumps of fat from rabbit pieces. Coat rabbit in seasoned flour; shake off excess.

Heat butter and oil in a wide skillet over medium-high heat. Add rabbit and cook until browned, 5 to 6 minutes on each side. Discard all but 1 tablespoon of pan drippings. Add shallot and cook 1 minute. Add 3/4 cup cider, cover and simmer until rabbit is tender when pierced with a fork, 35 to 40 minutes. Place rabbit on a serving platter.

If needed, add enough cider so there is 3/4 cup liquid in pan. Whisk in cream, mustard seeds, lemon peel and lemon juice. Cook until sauce thickens slightly. Add salt to taste. Pour over rabbit and sprinkle with parsley.

Makes 4 servings.

GLAZED GRILLED QUAIL

8 quail or 3 Rock Cornish game hens, rinsed
1/2 cup fresh orange juice
2 tablespoons brandy
2 tablespoons vegetable oil
1 garlic clove, minced
2 teaspoons grated orange peel
1 teaspoon dried rosemary
1/2 teaspoon each salt and pepper
1/3 cup red chile pepper jelly
Oranges and rosemary sprigs for garnish

Cut through breastbone of each quail with poultry shears; spread quail open, skin-side up, on a flat surface and press firmly to crack bones. If using game hens, cut through backbone and breastbone of each; cut out rest of backbone with poultry shears.

In a small bowl, combine juice, brandy, oil, garlic, peel, rosemary, salt and pepper. Place birds in a heavy plastic bag; add marinade and seal. Refrigerate 8 to 24 hours. Drain marinade into a bowl. Simmer 1/3 cup of marinade in a small pan over low heat 5 minutes. Add jelly and simmer until jelly melts. Reserve remaining marinade.

Preheat charcoal grill and grease rack. Place birds 4 to 6 inches above coals. Cook birds, turning frequently and basting with reserved marinade. Cook quail until breast meat is cooked through but still pink near bone (3 to 4 minutes per side). Cook game hens until meat near thighbone is no longer pink (15 to 18 minutes per side). During the last 2 or 3 minutes of cooking, brush with jelly marinade to glaze birds.

Makes 4 to 6 servings.

— FAJITAS WITH BELL PEPPERS —

5 tablespoons vegetable oil
3 tablespoons fresh lime juice
2 tablespoons each tequila and
   chopped onion
1 garlic clove, minced
1/2 fresh serrano chile, sliced crosswise
1/2 teaspoon ground cumin
1/4 teaspoon each dried leaf oregano, salt
   and pepper
1 beef flank steak (about 1-1/2 lbs.)
1/2 each green, red and yellow bell peppers,
   cut into thin strips
1 red onion, cut into 1/4-inch strips
8 to 12 (about 8-inch) flour tortillas
Dairy sour cream, lime wedges and salsa,
   to serve

Combine 3 tablespoons of the oil, the lime juice, tequila, chopped onion, garlic, chile, cumin, oregano, salt and pepper in a small bowl. Place meat in a heavy plastic bag, add marinade and seal bag. Refrigerate 8 to 48 hours.

When ready to cook, heat 1 tablespoon of the oil in a wide skillet over high heat; add bell peppers and red onion. Cook, stirring, until peppers are soft, 4 to 5 minutes. Cover and keep warm.

Drain meat; pat dry and rub off seasonings with paper towels. Heat the remaining oil in a wide skillet over medium-high heat. Add meat; cook until brown on both sides but still pink in center, 5 to 6 minutes total. To serve, cut meat across the grain into thin slanting slices; place in center of a warm platter. Place peppers and onion on ends of platter. Place tortillas and condiments in separate serving dishes. Wrap in tortillas to eat.

Makes 4 to 6 servings.

— TOSTADAS WITH PICADILLO —

1 tablespoon vegetable oil
1 small onion, chopped
1 garlic clove, minced
1 pound lean ground beef
2 medium-size tomatoes, peeled
    and chopped
2 tablespoons red-wine vinegar
1 tablespoon brown sugar
1/2 teaspoon ground cinnamon
1/4 teaspoon each ground cloves, ground
    cumin and salt
1/2 cup raisins, plumped in hot water 5 min-
    utes, drained
1/4 cup sliced pimento-stuffed green olives
2 cups Refried Beans (page 76) or 1 (about
    1-lb.) can refried beans
8 crisp-fried tortillas
2 cups shredded lettuce
1 cup (4 oz.) shredded Cheddar cheese
2 tomatoes, cut into wedges or chopped
1 cup Salsa Fresca (page 13)
Ripe olives and cilantro sprigs for garnish

Prepare Picadillo: Heat oil in a skillet over medium heat. Add onion; cook until soft but not brown, 4 to 5 minutes. Add garlic and beef. Cook, stirring, until meat is crumbly. Add peeled tomatoes, wine vinegar, sugar, spices and salt; cover and simmer 20 minutes. Add raisins and green olives; simmer, uncovered, 5 minutes.

Heat refried beans in a wide skillet. To assemble each tostada, place a tortilla on a dinner plate and spread with about 1/4 cup beans. Cover with pica-dillo, lettuce, cheese, tomatoes, salsa, ripe olives and cilantro.

Makes 8 tostadas.

— SOPAPILLAS WITH MEAT —

2 tablespoons vegetable oil
1/2 cup chopped onion
1 garlic clove, minced
1 teaspoon minced seeded fresh serrano chile
1-1/2 tablespoons all-purpose flour
1 cup chicken broth
1 (7-oz.) can whole green chiles, cut into
    1/2-inch pieces
1/8 teaspoon each ground cumin, dried leaf
    oregano and salt
6 Sopapillas shaped as 5" x 2-1/2" rectangles
    (page 93)
1-1/2 cups Machaca (page 60), Picadillo
    (opposite) or Carnitas (page 50), heated
1 cup (4 oz.) shredded Monterey Jack cheese
Chopped onion and cilantro, to serve

Preheat oven to 350F (175C). Prepare
Chile Verde: Heat oil in a 2-quart pan
over medium heat. Add onion, garlic
and fresh chile; cook until onion is soft.

Stir in flour and cook 1 minute. Whisk
in broth; cook, stirring, until sauce
thickens slightly. Add green chiles,
cumin, oregano and salt; simmer 2 minutes. Keep warm.

With a sharp knife, split each Sopapilla
in half; place bottom halves in a baking
pan. Spoon 1/4 cup meat filling into
each; sprinkle each with cheese. Replace
tops. Bake 10 minutes or until heated
through; cheese is melted. For each
serving, place a Sopapilla on a dinner
plate. Cover each with 1/4 cup Chile
Verde. Top with onion and cilantro.

Makes 6 servings.

TACOS DE MACHACA

2 pounds beef chuck roast
2 cups water
1/4 onion, sliced
8 black peppercorns
2 tablespoons vegetable oil
1 small onion, chopped
2 garlic cloves, minced
1 cup canned tomatoes, undrained
2 tablespoons canned diced green chile
1/2 teaspoon each ground cumin, dried leaf
    oregano and salt
8 corn tortillas
Guacamole (page 16) to serve

Prepare Machaca: Simmer meat, water, the 1/4 onion and peppercorns until very tender, about 2 hours; drain. Discard bone and fat; shred meat.

Heat oil in a wide skillet over medium heat. Add onion and garlic; cook until onion is soft, 4 to 5 minutes. Add meat and cook until lightly browned, 4 to 5 minutes. In a blender, puree tomatoes and chile with cumin, oregano and salt. Add to meat. Simmer until meat absorbs most of sauce, 15 to 20 minutes. Use half of Machaca for tacos; save remaining Machaca for other uses.

Wrap tortillas in foil; place in a 350F (175C) oven until softened, about 15 minutes. For each taco, place about 3 tablespoons of Machaca on a warm tortilla. Top with Guacamole. Fold in half and eat out of hand.

Makes 8 tacos.

FLAUTAS

12 corn tortillas
1-1/2 cups machaca (opposite)
Vegetable oil for deep-frying
Lettuce, radishes and dairy sour cream,
  to serve

Chipotle Salsa:
1/2 pound tomatillos, husks removed
1 tablespoon vegetable oil
1/4 cup chopped onion
2 garlic cloves, minced
2 tablespoons chopped cilantro
1 tablespoon chopped chiles chipotle en
  escabeche

Prepare salsa: In a small pan, simmer tomatillos in water 10 minutes or until tender; drain, reserving 1/3 cup of the liquid. Heat oil in a small skillet over medium heat. Add onion and garlic and cook until onion is soft, 4 to 5 minutes. In a blender, process tomatillos, reserved liquid, onion mixture, cilantro and chipotle chiles until smooth. Cover and refrigerate until ready to use.

For each Flauta, heat a tortilla in an ungreased skillet over medium-high heat 1 minute to soften. Place 2 tablespoons of machaca across center of tortilla. Tightly roll tortilla; secure open edge with a wooden pick.

Heat 1-1/2 inches oil in a skillet to 365F (185C). Fry Flautas, 2 or 3 at a time, until golden, but not too crisp, 1-1/2 to 2 minutes. Lift out with a slotted spoon; drain on paper towels. Remove wooden picks. Serve 2 or 3 flautas per person. Top with sour cream and chipotle salsa. Garnish with radishes.

Makes 12 Flautas.

Texas Brisket

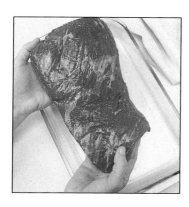

1 (4- to 5-lb.) beef brisket
2 tablespoons packed brown sugar
2 tablespoons cracked black pepper
2 tablespoons ground mild red chile
2 teaspoons ground cumin
1 teaspoon each salt and dried leaf oregano
1/2 teaspoon red (cayenne) pepper
1/4 cup canned beef broth
2 tablespoons fresh lime juice
2 teaspoons liquid smoke
1 cup bottled barbecue sauce

Trim and discard excess fat from meat; place meat in a 13" × 9" glass baking dish or other non-reactive dish in which the meat will fit snugly.

In a bowl, combine brown sugar, black pepper, ground chile, cumin, salt, oregano and cayenne; mix well. Stir in beef broth, lime juice and liquid smoke. Pour over meat; turn meat to coat. Cover tightly with foil and refrigerate at least 24 hours or up to 36 hours.

Preheat oven to 300F (150C). Bake meat 4 hours or until very tender when pierced with a fork. Remove meat from oven and let stand 10 minutes. Transfer meat to a cutting board; cover to keep warm. Skim fat from pan drippings. Pour drippings into a small pan; stir in barbecue sauce. Simmer 5 minutes. Slice meat across the grain and arrange on a platter. Drizzle sauce over meat.

Makes 10 to 12 servings.

ENCHILADAS VERDES

1/2 pound tomatillos, husks removed
1 tablespoon vegetable oil
1 small onion, chopped
1/4 cup slivered blanched almonds
1/4 cup canned diced green chiles
1 cup chicken broth
Salt
Vegetable oil for frying
8 corn tortillas
2 cups shredded cooked chicken
1-1/2 cups shredded Monterey Jack cheese
1/2 cup dairy sour cream

Prepare sauce: In a 2-quart pan, simmer tomatillos in water 10 minutes or until tender; drain. Heat oil in a medium-size skillet over medium heat. Add onion and cook until soft but not brown, 4 to 5 minutes. Add almonds and cook 2 minutes. In a blender, process tomatillos, onion mixture, chiles and broth until smooth. Add salt to taste. Return to skillet; simmer until sauce is thickened.

Preheat oven to 350F (175C). Heat 1/2 inch oil in a small skillet over medium-high heat. Place 1 tortilla in oil; cook 2 seconds on each side or just until limp. Lift out with tongs, drain briefly, then dip into sauce.

Transfer sauced tortilla to a plate. Place about 1/4 cup chicken and 2 tablespoons of the cheese across center of tortilla; roll up and place in a baking dish. Repeat. Pour remaining sauce over enchiladas; reserve remaining cheese. Cover and bake 20 minutes or until heated through. Sprinkle with cheese. Bake, uncovered, 10 minutes or until cheese is melted. Spoon sour cream down center of enchiladas.

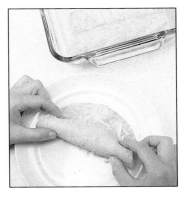

Makes 4 servings.

CHICKEN CHIMICHANGAS

2 tablespoons vegetable oil
1 small onion, chopped
2 garlic cloves, minced
1 (4-oz.) can diced green chiles
1/2 teaspoon ground cumin
2 cups shredded cooked chicken
6 (10- to 12-inch) flour tortillas
2 small tomatoes, diced
1 cup (4 oz.) shredded Monterey Jack cheese
Vegetable oil for deep-frying
Tomatillo Salsa (page 15), to serve

Heat oil in a wide skillet over medium heat. Add onion and cook until soft but not brown, 4 to 5 minutes. Stir in garlic, chiles, cumin and chicken; cook about 1 minute.

To make each chimichanga, place 1/6 of chicken mixture in center of each tortilla; top with about 2 tablespoons of the tomato and 2 tablespoons of the cheese. Fold in sides to partially enclose filling; fold lower edge over part of filling, then roll to form a tight cylinder. Secure open edge with a wooden pick.

Heat 1 inch oil in a large skillet until a 1-inch bread cube turns golden-brown in 65 seconds. One at a time, cook chimichangas, 1 minute or until golden. Turn over; continue cooking 1 minute or until golden. Lift out with a slotted spatula and drain on paper towels. Keep warm in a 200F (95C) oven until all chimichangas are cooked. Remove wooden picks before serving. Serve with salsa.

Makes 6 chimichangas.

— Chicken Breast Rellenos —

6 boneless skinless chicken breast halves
1 each small carrot and zucchini, cut into
   3-inch matchstick pieces
18 pitted ripe olives
1 cup canned enchilada sauce
3 tablespoons vegetable oil
2 thin slices jicama, cut into 3-inch matchstick pieces
1 (3" x 2") piece red bell pepper, cut into
   3-inch matchstick pieces
2 greens onions, cut into 3-inch slivers

Remove the fillet (small muscle) from each chicken breast half; reserve for other uses. Split each breast half horizontally almost all the way through; open it up like a book. Place breast halves between waxed paper; pound to an even thickness.

On each of 6 carrot pieces, thread 3 olives. Whisk together chile sauce and oil. Brush a chicken breast on both sides with sauce; place sauced breast, cut-side up, on a work surface. Place a carrot stick with olives on one wide end of breast; top with 1/6 of carrot, jicama, zucchini, bell pepper and green onions. Roll up breast. Place roll, seam-side down, in a 13" × 9" baking pan. Repeat until all breasts are rolled. Brush again with sauce.

Preheat oven to 350F (175C). Bake rolls, uncovered, until juices run clear when chicken is pierced with a fork, 30 to 35 minutes. Brush with pan juices several times during baking. Serve chicken breasts whole or sliced.

Makes 6 servings.

— GRILLED TURKEY ADOVADA —

3 tablespoons fresh orange juice
2 tablespoons olive oil
2 teaspoons ground mild red chile
2 garlic cloves, minced
1/2 teaspoon each dried leaf oregano and salt
1/4 teaspoon each ground cumin and pepper
3 turkey breast fillets or tenderloins (1-1/4 lbs. total)

Cranberry Salsa:
1-1/2 cups fresh or frozen cranberries
2 tablespoons each minced red onion and cilantro
2 tablespoons each honey and fresh orange juice
1/4 orange (with peel), chopped
1 fresh jalapeño or serrano chile, seeded and minced
Salt

In a plastic bag, combine orange juice, oil, ground chile, garlic, oregano, salt, cumin and pepper. Add turkey; seal bag. Refrigerate 2 hours.

Prepare salsa: In a bowl combine cranberries, onion, cilantro, honey, orange juice, orange, fresh chile and salt. Cover and refrigerate until ready to use.

Preheat charcoal grill and grease rack. Lift turkey from marinade; reserve marinade. Place turkey 4 to 6 inches above coals. Cook, turning frequently and basting with reserved marinade, until meat is white in center of thickest part, 8 to 10 minutes. Cut fillets cross-wise in 1/2-inch slanting slices and serve with salsa.

Makes 4 servings.

TURKEY TAMALE PIE

1 tablespoon vegetable oil
1 small onion, chopped
1/2 cup diced green bell pepper
1 garlic clove, minced
1 (about 1-lb.) can tomatoes, undrained
2 cups diced cooked turkey
1 cup cooked whole-kernel corn
1/2 cup pitted ripe olives
2 tablespoons ground mild red chile
1/2 teaspoon each ground cumin, dried leaf
    oregano and salt

Cornmeal Topping:
1/2 cup yellow cornmeal
1-1/2 cups milk
2 tablespoons butter or margarine
2 large eggs, lightly beaten
1 cup (4 oz.) shredded Cheddar cheese
1/2 teaspoon salt

Preheat oven to 375F (190C). Heat oil in a wide skillet over medium heat. Add onion, bell pepper and garlic; cook until onion is soft but not brown. Cut up tomatoes; add to pan with liquid, turkey, corn, olives, ground chile, cumin, oregano and salt. Simmer 10 minutes. Turn into a shallow 2-quart casserole dish.

Combine cornmeal and 1/2 cup of the milk. Scald remaining milk over medium heat. Stir in cornmeal mixture; cook, stirring, until cornmeal is thick, 3 to 4 minutes. Add butter. Stir a little of hot cornmeal into eggs. Return to pan and mix well. Stir in cheese and salt.

Spoon cornmeal mixture over turkey. Bake until a knife inserted in center of topping comes out clean, 45 minutes.

Makes 6 servings.

RED PEPPER FETTUCCINE

2 cups all-purpose flour
2 large eggs
2 to 3 teaspoons red pepper flakes
4 tablespoons water

Place flour, eggs and pepper flakes in a food processor; process until mixture looks like cornmeal. With motor running, add water and process until dough forms a ball. If dough is crumbly, add 1 or 2 teaspoons water. Knead on a floured board until smooth and elastic, 3 minutes. Cover for 20 minutes.

Cut dough into 4 portions. Flatten slightly; dust with flour, then feed through widest roller setting on pasta machine. Fold dough into thirds and feed through rollers. Repeat folding and rolling process 4 times or until dough is elastic.

Set rollers one notch closer together and feed dough through. Repeat the rolling, setting rollers closer each time, until dough has been fed through the next to last setting. Cut strip in half crosswise for easy handling. Let strips dry until leathery but pliable, 5 to 10 minutes, then cut using medium-wide blades. Lightly flour cut noodles to keep strands separate. Leave uncovered up to 1 hour before cooking. Cook in boiling salted water until tender yet firm to the bite, 2 to 3 minutes.

Makes about 4 cups cooked fettuccine.

Variation
Jalapeño Fettuccine: Substitute 2 minced seeded fresh jalapeño chiles for red pepper flakes. Reduce water to 3-1/2 tablespoons.

PASTA WITH SOUTHWEST PESTO

1 cup packed fresh basil leaves
1/4 cup packed cilantro
1/4 cup grated Parmesan cheese
2 tablespoons pine nuts
1 garlic clove, cut in thirds
1/3 cup olive oil
1 tablespoon fresh lemon juice
Jalapeño Fettuccine (opposite) or 8 ounces
    packaged fettuccine, cooked and drained
Basil sprigs for garnish

Place basil, cilantro, cheese, nuts and garlic in a food processor; process to make a paste. Add oil and lemon juice; process briefly to blend.

If not using at once, spoon into an airtight container, cover and refrigerate up to 3 days. To serve, pour over hot fettuccine and toss. Garnish with basil.

Makes 4 servings.

– Pasta & Red Pepper Pesto –

1/2 cup roasted red bell pepper
1/4 cup canned diced green chiles
2 tablespoons grated Parmesan cheese
2 tablespoons pumpkin seeds, toasted
1 tablespoon chopped cilantro
2 tablespoons olive oil
1 teaspoon lemon juice
Salt, to taste
Red Pepper Fettuccine (page 68) or 8 ounces
   packaged fettuccine, cooked and drained
Additional pumpkin seeds for garnish

Place bell pepper, green chiles, cheese, 2 tablespoons pumpkin seeds and cilantro in a food processor; process to make a paste. Add oil and lemon juice; process briefly to blend. Add salt.

If not using at once, spoon into an air-tight container, cover and refrigerate up to 3 days. To serve, pour over hot fettuccine and toss. Garnish with additional pumpkin seeds.

Makes 4 servings.

FLAT BLUE ENCHILADAS

1 cup Red Chile Sauce I (page 74) or Red
   Chile Sauce II (page 75)
6 blue cornmeal crepes (page 21)
1-1/2 cups (6 ounces) shredded longhorn
   cheese or mild Cheddar cheese
1/2 cup chopped red onion
Shredded lettuce for garnish

Preheat oven to 300F (150C). In a pan,
heat chile sauce. Have ready 2 ovenproof dinner plates. To assemble each
enchilada, spoon a thin layer of sauce
on plate; cover with 1 crepe.

Coat crepe with a thin layer of sauce,
then sprinkle with cheese and onion.
Repeat this layering with 2 more crepes.

When both stacks are completed, pour
any remaining sauce over the stacks
and sprinkle with any remaining
cheese. Bake 10 minutes or until enchiladas are heated through and cheese
has melted. Garnish with lettuce.

Makes 2 servings.

Variation
*Add 1 cup shredded cooked chicken and
reduce cheese to 1 cup.*

Enchiladas Coloradas

1-1/2 cups (6 oz.) each shredded Monterey
   Jack and mild Cheddar cheeses
1 (6- to 8-oz.) can pitted ripe olives, drained
2 cups Carnitas (page 50), shredded; Machaca
   (page 60); or shredded cooked chicken
2 cups Red Chile Sauce I (page 74) or Red
   Chile Sauce II (page 75)
Vegetable oil for frying
12 corn tortillas

Preheat oven to 350F (175C). Mix
cheeses together. Thickly slice 12 olives
and set aside. Chop remaining olives
and mix with meat. In a pan, heat the
chile sauce.

Heat 1/2 inch oil in a small skillet over
medium-high heat. Place 1 tortilla in
oil; cook 2 seconds on each side or just
until limp. Lift out with tongs; drain
briefly, then dip in chile sauce. Transfer
sauced tortilla to a plate. Place a scant 3
tablespoons meat mixture and 2 tablespoons of cheese across center of tortilla; roll up and place in a baking dish.
Repeat with remaining tortillas.

When all enchiladas are prepared, pour
remaining chile sauce over enchiladas;
reserve remaining cheese and sliced
olives. Cover baking dish with foil.
Bake 20 minutes or until heated
through. Uncover and sprinkle with
reserved cheese; scatter olives over the
cheese. Continue baking, uncovered, 10
minutes or until cheese is melted.

Makes 6 servings.

— CHEESE & CHILE TAMALES —

36 dried corn husks
2 cups masa harina (dehydrated masa flour)
2/3 cup solid vegetable shortening
1/2 teaspoon each baking powder and salt
1-1/3 cups lukewarm chicken broth
8 ounces Monterey Jack cheese, cut into
   24 cubes
1 (4-oz.) can diced green chiles, drained
Salsa Fresca (page 13)

Cover husks with warm water and let stand until pliable, 2 to 24 hours. Process masa harina, shortening, baking powder and salt in a food processor until mixture looks like cornmeal. With motor running, pour broth down feed tube and process until dough is light and fluffy, 1 to 2 minutes. Rinse husks and remove any silks; drain well. Sort through husks and select 24 that are at least 4 inches across at the base for tamales; tear extra husks into thin strips.

Spread 1 husk out flat; using a small spatula or your fingers, spread 1 tablespoon dough in center near wide end of husk. Place 1 cheese cube and a few diced chiles in center of dough. Top with another tablespoon of dough; spread to cover filling. Fold sides of husk over dough, then fold pointed end of husk down over filled end. With a strip of husk, tie tamale to hold shut. Repeat to make 23 more tamales.

Stand tamales on folded ends in a steamer or on a rack over at least 1 inch water in a large pot. Cover and steam 1 hour (add boiling water to steamer as needed) or until dough is firm and pulls away easily from husk.

Makes 24 tamales, 6 to 8 servings.

RED CHILE SAUCE I

10 dried red New Mexican chiles
2 dried ancho (pasilla) chiles
3-1/2 cups water
2 tablespoons vegetable oil
1/4 cup minced onion
1 garlic clove, minced
1 tablespoon all-purpose flour
1 teaspoon salt
1/4 teaspoon each ground cumin and dried
    leaf oregano

Rinse chiles. In a dry skillet over medium-low heat, toast chiles, turning frequently, until they smell toasty, 3 to 4 minutes. Discard stems and seeds. Place in a medium-size pan with the water and simmer 20 minutes or until chiles are soft.

Pour chiles and liquid into a blender or food processor; process until pureed. Push puree through a wire strainer; discard residue.

Heat oil in a wide skillet over medium heat. Add onion and garlic and cook until onion is soft, 4 to 5 minutes. Add flour and cook 1 minute. Add chile puree, salt, cumin and oregano, and cook, stirring constantly, until sauce comes to a boil. Reduce heat and simmer 2 minutes. Let sauce cool, then cover and refrigerate up to 3 days or freeze for longer storage.

Makes 2-1/2 cups.

Red Chile Sauce II

2 tablespoons vegetable oil
1/4 cup minced onion
1 garlic clove, minced
2 tablespoons all-purpose flour
1/3 cup ground mild red chile
1/2 teaspoon salt
1/4 teaspoon each ground cumin and dried
    leaf oregano
2 cups water

Heat oil in a 2-quart pan over medium heat. Add onion and garlic, and cook until onion is soft, 4 to 5 minutes. Add flour and cook 1 minute.

Stir in ground chile, salt, cumin and oregano. Add water and cook, stirring constantly, until the sauce is thick and boiling.

Reduce heat to simmer and cook 5 minutes. Let sauce cool, then cover and refrigerate up to 3 days or freeze.

Makes 2 cups.

FRIJOLES

1 pound dried pinto, red, pink or black beans
6 cups water
1 medium-size onion, chopped
2 garlic cloves, minced
2 tablespoons vegetable oil
1 teaspoon salt or to taste

Pick over beans and discard any pebbles, broken beans or beans that are shriveled or discolored. Rinse beans under cold running water.

Place beans in a large kettle. Add enough water to cover beans by 2 inches. Cover and let stand overnight. Or cover and bring to a boil. Boil 2 minutes. Turn off heat and let stand, covered, 1 hour. Drain beans and add the 6 cups water. Add onion, garlic and oil. Boil 10 minutes. Reduce heat. Simmer, with lid ajar, until beans are tender, 1-1/2 to 2 hours for pinto, red or pink beans, 2-1/2 hours for black beans. Add water as necessary. During the last 30 minutes of cooking, add salt.

Makes 6 cups.

Variation
Refried Beans: *Remove 4 cups beans with a slotted spoon. Process beans in a food processor or mash with a potato masher. Heat 2 tablespoons vegetable oil in a wide skillet. Add mashed beans and cook over medium heat until beans cook into a thick paste. If too dry, stir in small amounts of bean broth. Top with 1 cup shredded Cheddar cheese. Makes 4 to 6 servings.*

Cowboy Beans

1 pound dried pinto beans, sorted, rinsed
   and drained
8 cups water
1 (1-1/2-lb.) ham shank
2 medium-size onions, chopped
2 garlic cloves, minced
1 teaspoon ground cumin
1 teaspoon dried leaf oregano
1/2 teaspoon pepper
1 teaspoon salt
2 limes

Place beans in a large kettle. Add
enough water to cover beans by 2 inches. Cover and let stand overnight. Or
cover and bring to a boil. Boil 2 minutes. Turn off heat and let stand, covered, 1 hour.

Drain beans, and add the 8 cups water.
Add ham shank, onions and garlic. Boil
10 minutes. Reduce heat. Simmer, with
lid ajar, 2 hours. Remove shank; cut
meat into bite-size pieces.

Return meat to pan and add cumin,
oregano and pepper. Continue to simmer until beans are very tender, about 1
more hour. At end of cooking, beans
should have a little liquid. If beans
become dry, add more water. If beans
are too soupy, continue to cook, stirring
occasionally, until desired consistency.
Add salt to taste starting with 1 teaspoon. Cut limes into wedges; pass at
the table to squeeze over each serving.

Makes 6 to 8 servings.

Green Chile Risotto

2 tablespoons olive oil
1-1/2 tablespoons achiote seeds
1 tablespoon butter or margarine
1 medium-size onion, chopped
1 garlic clove, minced
1-1/2 cups short-grain white rice
4-1/2 cups chicken broth
1/4 cup diced green chiles
1/4 cup grated Parmesan cheese
Parmesan cheese shavings for garnish

Place oil and achiote seeds in a 3-quart pan; cook over low heat until seeds turn very dark red and oil is a deep red color. Pour oil and seeds into a sieve lined with cheesecloth and placed over a bowl. Discard seeds; return oil to pan.

Add butter and onion. Cook, stirring frequently, over medium heat until onion is soft and golden, 4 to 5 minutes. Add garlic and rice and stir until rice is opaque, 3 to 4 minutes.

Add broth. Cook, uncovered, stirring occasionally, until broth comes to a boil. Adjust heat so rice boils gently; cook, uncovered, until rice is tender yet firm and most of liquid is absorbed, 20 to 25 minutes. Turn off heat and stir in chiles and Parmesan cheese. Serve at once or cover pan to keep risotto warm up to 15 minutes. Garnish with cheese shavings.

Makes 6 servings.

— Mexican Cinnamon Rice —

2 tablespoons butter or margarine
1/2 cup chopped onion
1/3 cup shredded carrot
1/3 cup diced celery
1-1/2 cups long-grain white rice
1-1/2 teaspoons ground cinnamon
1/2 teaspoon ground coriander
3 cups chicken broth
1/3 cup currants or raisins
2 tablespoons chopped parsley
Carrot shreds and celery leaves for garnish

Melt butter in a 2- to 3-quart pan over medium-low heat. Add onion, carrot and celery. Cover pan; cook until onion is soft but not brown, 6 to 7 minutes.

Add rice, cinnamon and coriander, and cook, stirring, 2 minutes or until rice is coated with butter. Add chicken broth. Cover and bring to a boil, then reduce heat and simmer until rice is tender yet firm and liquid is absorbed, about 20 minutes.

Stir in currants and parsley; fluff rice with a fork. Cover and let stand 5 minutes. Garnish with carrot shreds and celery leaves.

Makes 6 servings.

PICO DE GALLO

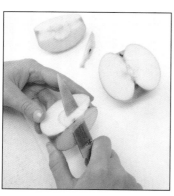

1 small jicama
6 to 8 small tomatillos
2 oranges
1 Granny Smith apple
2 limes
Salt
Ground mild red chile
2 tablespoons chopped cilantro

Cut jicama in half; place, flat-side down, on work surface and cut into 1/4-inch-thick slices. Pull off brown skin. Stack slices, a few at a time, and cut crosswise into 1/4-inch sticks. Remove papery husks from tomatillos and wash. Cut uncored tomatillos crosswise into 1/4-inch-thick slices.

Peel oranges; quarter lengthwise. Cut each section crosswise into 1/4-inch-thick slices. Quarter unpeeled apple; remove core. Place apple wedges, flat-side down, on work surface and cut crosswise in 1/4-inch-thick slices. Squeeze juice of 1/2 lime over slices. Cut remaining 1-1/2 limes into wedges.

In a serving bowl, arrange in separate piles, jicama, tomatillos, oranges and apple. Sprinkle lightly with salt and ground chile. Sprinkle with cilantro. Garnish with lime wedges.

Makes 6 to 8 servings.

CREAMY COLE SLAW

1/2 small head green cabbage
1/2 small head red cabbage
1 small Granny Smith apple, quartered and
    thinly sliced crosswise
1/4 cup chopped green bell pepper
1/4 cup finely chopped red onion
2 green onions (including tops), thinly sliced
Salt
Apple slices, to garnish

Creamy Dressing:
1/4 cup mayonnaise
1/4 cup dairy sour cream
1/4 cup sweet pickle juice
1 tablespoon white-wine vinegar
1 teaspoon celery seeds
1 teaspoon mustard seeds
2 to 4 drops hot pepper sauce

To prepare dressing: In a medium-size bowl, whisk together mayonnaise, sour cream, pickle juice, wine vinegar, celery seeds, mustard seeds and hot sauce until smooth.

Cut each cabbage half lengthwise into 2 wedges; slice off and discard cores. Place each wedge, flat-side down, on a cutting board; thinly slice crosswise to make fine shreds.

Place cabbage in a large bowl. Add apple, bell pepper, red onion and green onions. Add dressing and toss to evenly coat. Add salt to taste and mix again. Cover and refrigerate at least 1 hour for flavors to blend. Turn into a serving container and garnish with apple slices.

Makes 6 servings (4 cups).

ZUCCHINI SALAD

1-1/2 pounds slender green and yellow zucchini, cut into 1/4-inch-thick slices
1 cup thinly sliced celery
1/2 cup canned nopalitos, drained and diced
1 (4-oz.) can whole green chiles, drained and cut into 1/2-inch pieces
1/2 cup pimento-stuffed green olives, each cut into thirds
1/3 cup thinly sliced green onions
1 small avocado
Lettuce leaves
3 ounces feta cheese, crumbled

Cumin Vinaigrette:
3 tablespoons olive oil
2 tablespoons white-wine vinegar
1/2 teaspoon salt
1/4 teaspoon each ground cumin, garlic powder and ground mild red chile
1/8 teaspoon pepper

To prepare dressing: In a small bowl, whisk oil, vinegar, salt, cumin, garlic powder, ground chile and pepper.

In a large skillet, cook zucchini, covered, in 1 inch boiling water until crisp-tender, 2 to 3 minutes; drain. Rinse with cold water and drain again; pat dry with paper towels. Place zucchini in a large bowl with celery, nopalitos, green chiles, olives and green onions. Add dressing and stir gently with a rubber spatula. Cover and refrigerate 1 hour.

Just before serving, dice avocado. Fold into salad. Serve in a large bowl lined with lettuce leaves. Sprinkle cheese over top.

Makes 6 to 8 serving (6 cups).

TEXAS CAVIAR

1 (15-oz.) can black-eyed peas
1 (1-lb.) can black beans
2/3 cup diced jicama, cut into 1/4-inch pieces
3 green onions (including tops), thinly sliced
1 tablespoon minced fresh jalapeño or
    serrano chile
2 tablespoons chopped cilantro
1/2 small red onion
Red leaf lettuce

Chile Dressing:
1/4 cup vegetable oil
2 tablespoons red-wine vinegar
1 garlic clove, minced
1/2 teaspoon ground mild red chile
1/2 teaspoon dried leaf oregano
1/2 teaspoon salt
1/4 teaspoon pepper

To prepare dressing: In a bowl, whisk together oil, wine vinegar, garlic, ground chile, oregano, salt and pepper.

Drain black-eyed peas and beans in a colander. Rinse with cold water and drain again. In a large bowl, combine black-eyed peas, beans, jicama, green onions, fresh chile and cilantro. Pour over dressing; stir until evenly mixed. Cover and refrigerate at least 1 hour for flavors to blend.

Thinly slice red onion and separate into rings. Place in a bowl of salted water; cover and refrigerate 1 hour. Line a serving bowl with lettuce leaves. Spoon salad into bowl. Drain onion rings and place on top of salad.

Makes 6 servings (4 cups).

– RANCH-STYLE POTATO SALAD –

2 pounds thin-skinned, small red potatoes
8 bacon slices, crisp-cooked and crumbled
1 cup thinly sliced celery
1 cup shredded carrot
1 cup sliced green onions (including tops)

Dressing:
1/4 cup mayonnaise
2 tablespoons white-wine vinegar
2 tablespoons prepared mustard
1 tablespoon prepared horseradish
1/2 teaspoon ground turmeric
1/3 cup vegetable oil

To prepare Dressing: In a medium-size bowl, whisk together mayonnaise, wine vinegar, mustard, horseradish and turmeric until smooth. Add oil and whisk until evenly blended.

In a 5-quart pan, cook unpeeled potatoes in 1-1/2 inches boiling water until tender when pierced with a fork, 20 to 30 minutes; drain. Return pan to low heat and shake 2 or 3 minutes or until all moisture is evaporated. When cool enough to handle, cut potatoes into quarters or smaller, according to size. Place in a large bowl. Add dressing; stir with a rubber spatula until potatoes are well coated. Let stand 1 hour.

When potatoes are cool, add bacon, celery, carrot and green onions. Stir until evenly mixed. Let stand at least 30 minutes for flavors to blend. Spoon into a serving bowl.

Makes 8 servings (8 cups).

– TOMATO-TOMATILLO SALAD –

2 pounds (6 cups) mixed red and yellow cherry tomatoes or small (1/2 inch or less in
  diameter) pear-shaped tomatoes
1/2 pound small tomatillos
1/2 cup chopped red onion

Dressing:
6 tablespoons olive oil
2 tablespoons balsamic vinegar
2 tablespoons white-wine vinegar
1/2 teaspoon salt
1/4 teaspoon pepper
1/4 teaspoon paprika
3 tablespoons chopped fresh basil

Remove stems from tomatoes and discard; rinse and drain. Cut large tomatoes in half.

Remove papery husks from tomatillos;
rinse and drain. Cut into 1/4-inch
wedges. Place tomatoes in a wide shallow salad bowl with tomatillos and
red onion.

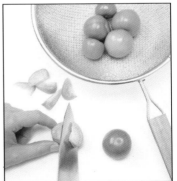

To prepare Dressing: In a bowl, whisk
together oil, vinegars, salt, pepper and
paprika. Pour over salad and mix gently. Sprinkle with basil.

Makes 8 servings (8 cups).

GUAYMAS FRUIT SALAD

1 small pineapple, cut into short spears
1 cantaloupe, cut into crescents
1 papaya, cut into crescents
1 mango, cut lengthwise into 12 pieces
3 kiwifruit, thinly sliced

Chile-Fruit Dressing:
1/2 cup dairy sour cream
1/2 cup fresh orange juice
2 tablespoons fresh lime juice
1/4 cup honey
1/4 cup vegetable oil
2 teaspoons ground mild red chile
1/4 teaspoon salt

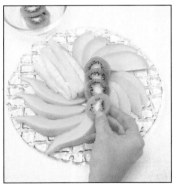

Arrange fruit on a large platter; cover and refrigerate until ready to serve.

To prepare dressing: In a blender or food processor, blend sour cream, orange juice, lime juice, honey, oil, ground chile and salt until smooth. Pour into a small pitcher; cover and refrigerate 1 hour for flavors to blend. Pass dressing at the table to pour over the fruit.

Makes 8 servings.

CHILE ONION RINGS

2 large mild onions
1 cup milk
1 cup water
1 tablespoon ground mild red chile
1 teaspoon salt
1 cup all-purpose flour
Vegetable oil for deep-frying

Peel onions and cut crosswise into 1/4-inch-thick slices. Place in a 13" × 9" glass pan. Pour milk and water over onions. Let stand 30 minutes. In a small bowl, combine ground chile and salt; set aside.

When ready to cook, pour oil into a deep 2-1/2- to 3-quart pan and heat to 360F (180C). Place flour in a bag. Drain onions and separate into rings. A portion at a time, add onions to flour and shake to coat; place in a colander and shake to remove excess flour.

Add onions to oil, a handful at a time, and cook until golden-brown, 2 to 3 minutes. Remove from oil with a slotted spoon and drain on paper towels. Sprinkle lightly with chile mixture. Serve warm. If made ahead, spread in a single layer in a shallow baking pan lined with paper towels. Heat in a 300F (150C) oven 4 to 5 minutes.

Makes 4 servings.

ZUCCHINI-CORN CAKES

1/2 cup yellow cornmeal
1/4 cup all-purpose flour
1/4 teaspoon baking soda
1/2 teaspoon ground cumin
1/4 teaspoon salt
1/4 teaspoon pepper
1 medium-size (6- or 7-oz.) zucchini
1 egg, beaten
3/4 cup buttermilk
1-1/2 tablespoons vegetable oil
1/2 cup fresh or canned whole-kernel corn
1 green onion (including top), minced
About 1 tablespoon butter or margarine
Dairy sour cream

In a large bowl, stir together cornmeal, flour, soda, cumin, salt and pepper.

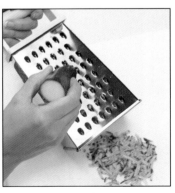

Using large holes on a shredder, shred zucchini to make 3/4 cup (pack in cup to measure). Squeeze with your hands to extract excess moisture. In a medium-size bowl, mix egg, buttermilk, oil, zucchini, corn and green onion. Pour liquid into dry ingredients and stir until evenly moistened.

Preheat a large skillet over medium-high heat. Grease lightly with butter. Spoon about 2 tablespoons batter onto skillet for each cake, spreading batter to make 3-inch cakes. Cook until tiny bubbles form in the centers and edges of cakes appear dry; turn and cook other sides until browned and cakes puff slightly. Serve 2 or 3 cakes per person. Top each serving with sour cream.

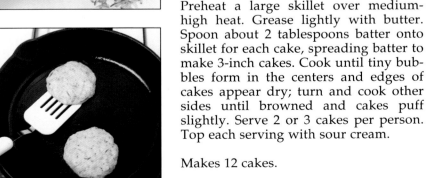

Makes 12 cakes.

SOUTHWEST RATATOUILLE

3 tablespoons olive oil
1 medium-size onion, coarsely chopped
1 medium-size eggplant, cut into
    1-inch cubes
2 garlic cloves, minced
1 fresh jalapeño chile, seeded and minced
2 medium-size chayotes (1 lb. total)
1 (about 1-lb.) can tomatoes, undrained
1 red bell pepper, cut into 3/4-inch pieces
1 teaspoon dried leaf basil
1/2 teaspoon dried leaf oregano
1/2 teaspoon salt
1/4 teaspoon pepper
1 (15-oz.) can baby corn, drained
2 tablespoons chopped parsley
1 tablespoon chopped cilantro

Heat oil in 5-quart pan over medium heat. Add onion and cook until soft but not brown, 4 to 5 minutes. Add eggplant, garlic and chile. Cook, stirring occasionally, 5 minutes. Quarter each chayote lengthwise, cutting through the seed. (When cooked it's edible.) Cut quarters crosswise into 1/4-inch slices.

Chop tomatoes; add to pan with juice. Add chayotes, bell pepper, herbs, salt and pepper. Bring to a boil. Cover, reduce heat and simmer 20 minutes. Add corn; cook until chayotes and eggplant are tender, 15 to 20 minutes. Stir occasionally.

Remove pan from heat. Tipping pan slightly and using a bulb baster, remove most of pan juices and place in a small pan. Cook over medium-high heat until liquid is syrupy and reduced to 1/3 cup. Pour over vegetables. Stir in parsley and cilantro. Serve hot or at room temperature.

Makes 6 to 8 servings.

GARLIC MASHED POTATOES

20 large garlic cloves
1 cup chicken broth
2-1/2 to 3 pounds russet potatoes, peeled
1 (3-oz.) package cream cheese, softened
1/2 cup dairy sour cream
2 to 3 tablespoons milk
1 (4-oz.) can diced green chiles, drained
1/4 teaspoon salt or to taste
2 tablespoons butter or margarine
Ground mild red chile

Place unpeeled garlic into a small pan with chicken broth. Cover and simmer until garlic is tender when pierced, 30 to 35 minutes. Drain, and if desired, save broth for other uses. Drop garlic into a sieve placed over a bowl; mash with a pestle or wooden spoon to make 2 tablespoons puree.

Cut potatoes into quarters. In a medium-size pan, cook potatoes, covered, in 1 inch water until tender, 20 to 25 minutes; drain. Using an electric mixer, beat hot potatoes until well mashed. Beat in cheese. Add garlic puree and sour cream; beat until fluffy and smooth. For more moist potatoes, beat in milk as desired. Stir in green chiles and salt.

Butter a shallow 2-quart casserole dish. Spoon potatoes into buttered dish. Dot with butter and sprinkle with ground chile. If made ahead, cover and refrigerate up to 24 hours. Preheat oven to 400F (205C). Bake, covered, 30 minutes; uncover and bake 10 to 15 more minutes or until top is golden-brown.

Makes 6 to 8 servings.

CORN TORTILLAS

2 cups masa harina (dehydrated masa flour)
1-1/4 to 1-1/2 cups warm water

Place masa harina in a large bowl; gradually work in water, mixing well and kneading 3 to 5 minutes. Break off a large walnut-size piece of dough and pat it 2 or 3 times to partially flatten; keep remaining dough covered with plastic wrap to prevent drying.

Place flattened dough on a tortilla press between a folded sheet of plastic wrap or waxed paper. Close the lid and press hard. Or with rolling pin, roll dough, placed between plastic wrap, into a 6- to 7-inch round. Peel off plastic wrap. If dough has the right amount of liquid, the plastic will peel easily off tortilla. If it cracks around the edges, add a little more water to dough and knead well.

Heat an ungreased heavy skillet over medium-high heat. Place a tortilla on hot skillet and cook until edge begins to dry, about 30 seconds. Turn and cook until lightly speckled on the other side, about 1 minute. Turn tortilla again and cook about 30 seconds. Stack cooked tortillas in an insulated tortilla warmer or covered dish and wrap in a clean towel to keep them soft and warm. Serve warm, or let cool, wrap airtight and refrigerate. To reheat, individually place in a heavy ungreased skillet and cook over medium heat 45 seconds on each side.

Makes 12 tortillas.

FLOUR TORTILLAS

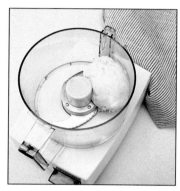

2 cups all-purpose flour
1/2 teaspoon salt
1/4 teaspoon baking powder
1/4 cup solid vegetable shortening
2/3 cup warm water

In a food processor, process flour, salt, baking powder and shortening until mixture resembles fine meal. With motor running, pour water down the feed tube and process until dough forms a ball. Or combine dry ingredients in a bowl; cut in shortening until mixture resembles fine crumbs. Stir in water with a fork. Turn dough onto a lightly floured board and knead until smooth, about 1 minute. Shape into a ball; cover with a bowl and let rest 30 minutes.

Divide dough into 8 equal portions for 8-inch tortillas, 12 portions for 6-inch tortillas; keep dough covered to prevent it from drying out. On a lightly floured board, roll out 1 portion at a time to make 1/8-inch-thick circles.

As each tortilla is shaped, place in preheated skillet. Cook 2 to 3 minutes on each side or until bubbly and browned. Stack cooked tortillas in an insulated tortilla warmer or covered dish or wrap in a clean towel to keep them soft and warm. Serve warm, or let cool, wrap airtight and refrigerate. To reheat, individually place in a heavy ungreased skillet and cook on medium heat 1 minute on each side.

Makes 8 large or 12 small tortillas.

SOPAPILLAS

2 cups all-purpose flour
2 teaspoons baking powder
1/2 teaspoon salt
1/2 teaspoon sugar
2 tablespoons solid vegetable shortening
3/4 cup warm water
Vegetable oil for deep-frying
Honey

In a food processor, process dry ingredients and shortening until mixture resembles fine meal. With motor running, pour water down feed tube; process until dough forms a ball. Or combine dry ingredients in a bowl; cut in shortening until mixture resembles fine crumbs. Stir in water. Turn dough onto a floured board and knead until smooth, about 1 minute.

Shape into a ball; cover with a bowl and let rest 30 minutes. Divide dough into 2 equal portions. With a rolling pin, roll each portion into a strip about 12 inches long, 2-1/2 inches wide and 1/8 inch thick; cut each strip into 8 triangles.

Pour oil into an electric skillet or deep heavy pan to a depth of 1-1/2 inches. Heat to 360F (180C). Cook 2 pieces at a time, turning once, until puffed and golden-brown, about 2 minutes. Lift out with a slotted spoon and drain on paper towels. Serve hot with honey.

Makes 16 sopapillas.

Variation
Sopapillas for stuffing: Divide dough into 12 equal portions; roll each portion into a 5" x 2-1/2" rectangle.

INDIAN FRY BREAD

2 cups all-purpose flour
1/4 cup nonfat dry milk powder
2 teaspoons baking powder
1/2 teaspoon salt
2 tablespoons solid vegetable shortening
3/4 cup warm water
Vegetable oil for deep-frying
Honey or powdered sugar, to serve

In a food processor, process dry ingredients and shortening until mixture resembles fine meal. With motor running, pour water down feed tube; process until dough forms a ball. Or combine dry ingredients in a bowl; cut in shortening until mixture resembles fine crumbs. Stir in water.

Turn dough onto a floured board and knead until smooth, about 1 minute. Shape into a ball; cover with a bowl and let rest 30 minutes. Divide dough into 8 equal portions; keep dough covered. One at a time, roll each portion into a ball; flatten slightly, then roll out to a circle about 7 inches in diameter and 1/8 inch thick. Poke a hole in center of round with your finger.

Pour oil into an electric skillet or deep heavy pan to a depth of 1-1/2 inches. Heat to 360F (180C). Cook rounds, 1 at a time, turning once, until puffed and golden-brown, about 2 minutes. Lift out with a slotted spoon and drain on paper towels. Serve with honey or sugar.

Makes 8 rounds.

Variation
Navajo Taco: *Top warm bread with beans or chili, lettuce, tomato and salsa.*

BLUE CORN CORNSTICKS

3/4 cup all-purpose flour
1/2 cup blue cornmeal
1-1/2 teaspoons baking powder
1/2 teaspoon sugar
1/4 teaspoon salt
1 large egg
3/4 cup milk
2-1/2 tablespoons vegetable oil
Butter for cooking

Piloncillo-Pecan Butter:
1 small cone piloncillo (Mexican raw sugar)
3 tablespoons water
1/2 cup butter or margarine, softened
1/4 cup very finely chopped pecans

Preheat oven to 400F (205C). Preheat cornstick pans in oven 5 minutes. In a medium-size bowl, stir together dry ingredients. In a small bowl, beat egg with milk and oil until blended. Pour liquid mixture into dry ingredients; stir just until moistened.

Heat 1/2 teaspoon butter in each section of cornstick pan; fill each section 3/4 full with batter. Bake until a wooden pick inserted in center comes out clean, 10 to 12 minutes for cornsticks.

Prepare butter: Using large holes of hand grater, grate piloncillo to make 1/4 cup. Place in a small pan with water. Cook, stirring occasionally, over low heat until piloncillo dissolves and mixture looks like warmed honey. Remove from heat and let cool. In a bowl, whip butter until fluffy. Add piloncillo syrup and nuts; whip until well blended.

Makes about 18 cornsticks.

JALAPEÑO CORN BREAD

8 bacon slices
1/2 cup chopped onion
3 or 4 fresh jalapeño or serrano chiles, seeded
and minced
1 cup all-purpose flour
1 cup yellow cornmeal
1 tablespoon baking powder
1/2 teaspoon salt
2 large eggs
1 cup milk
1/2 cup cooked whole-kernel corn
1/2 cup (2 oz.) shredded Cheddar cheese

Preheat oven to 400F (205C). Cook bacon in a skillet until crisp; drain on paper towels. Pour 2 tablespoons of the bacon drippings into a 9-inch cast-iron skillet or 9-inch-square baking pan. Discard all but 2 tablespoons of the remaining drippings. Add onion and chiles to remaining drippings in pan. Cook over medium heat until onion is soft but not brown, 4 to 5 minutes.

In a large bowl, combine dry ingredients. In a small bowl, beat eggs and milk. Crumble bacon; add bacon, onion mixture and corn to eggs. Pour mixture into dry ingredients; stir just until moistened.

Pour into skillet; sprinkle with cheese. Bake 20 to 25 minutes or until a wooden pick inserted in center comes out clean. Cut into wedges or squares; serve hot.

Makes 9 to 12 servings.

Mexican Spoonbread

4 tablespoons butter or margarine
1/2 cup chopped onion
1/3 cup chopped green and red bell peppers
2 fresh jalapeño chiles, seeded and minced
3/4 cup yellow cornmeal
2-1/4 cups milk
1 tablespoon sugar
1/2 teaspoon salt
3 large eggs, separated

Preheat oven to 350F (175C). Grease a 1-1/2-quart soufflé dish. Melt 2 tablespoons of the butter in a wide skillet over medium heat. Add onion, bell peppers and chiles; cook until onion is soft but not brown, 4 to 5 minutes.

In a small bowl, combine cornmeal and 1 cup of the milk. In a 2- to 3-quart pan, scald the remaining 1-1/4 cups milk over medium heat. Stir in moistened cornmeal; cook, stirring occasionally, until cornmeal is thickened, 3 to 4 minutes. Remove from heat and stir in the remaining 2 tablespoons butter. In a medium-size bowl, beat egg yolks slightly; stir in a little of the cornmeal mixture. Return yolks to hot cornmeal and mix well. Stir in onion mixture.

In a small bowl, beat egg whites until stiff. Fold 1/3 of whites into cornmeal mixture to lighten; fold in remaining egg whites until evenly blended. Spoon into prepared dish. Bake until puffed and a knife inserted in center comes out clean, 50 to 55 minutes. Serve immediately with a spoon.

Makes 6 servings.

CHILE-CHEESE BRIOCHES

1/2 cup warm water (110F, 45C)
1 (1/4-oz.) pkg. active dry yeast
1 tablespoon sugar
1-1/4 teaspoons salt
1/2 teaspoon ground mild red chile
3 large eggs
1/2 cup butter or margarine, cut into small pieces, softened
About 4 cups all-purpose flour
1/2 cup grated Asiago cheese or Parmesan cheese
1 (4-oz.) can diced green chiles, drained and patted dry with paper towels
1 egg yolk beaten with 1 tablespoon milk

In large bowl of an electric mixer, combine water and yeast; let stand 5 minutes to soften. Add sugar, salt, ground chile and eggs. Beat on low speed until mixed. Add butter, 3-1/2 cups of the flour and the cheese. Beat until dough holds together. (Dough will be soft.)

Turn dough onto a well-floured board. Sprinkle with half of the green chiles; fold dough in half and sprinkle with remaining chiles. Knead until chiles are evenly mixed and dough is smooth and satiny, 5 to 6 minutes; add flour as needed to prevent sticking. Grease a medium-size bowl. Turn dough over in greased bowl; cover and let rise in a warm place until doubled, 1 to 2 hours.

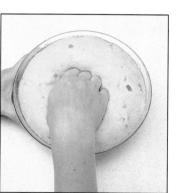

Punch dough down; knead briefly on floured board. Return to greased bowl; turn over to grease top. Cover with plastic wrap; refrigerate 12 to 24 hours.

Knead on floured board to expel air. Divide dough into 12 equal portions if using 3-inch muffin cups; 16 equal portions if using 2-1/2-inch muffin cups. Dough is easiest to handle if kept cold, so shape a few brioches at a time, keeping remaining dough covered and refrigerated. Butter muffin cups.

To shape each brioche, pinch off about 1/6 of each portion; set aside. Shape large section into a smooth ball by pulling surface of dough to underside of ball. Place ball, smooth-side up, in a buttered muffin cup; press dough down to evenly fill muffin cup. Shape the small piece of dough into a smooth teardrop. With your finger, poke a hole in center of brioche dough and securely insert pointed end of teardrop in hole. Repeat until all brioches are shaped.

Cover filled pans and let stand in a warm place until almost doubled, 1 to 1-1/2 hours. With a pastry brush, paint tops of brioches with egg-yolk mixture, being sure glaze does not accumulate in seams of topknots. Preheat oven to 425F (220C). Bake 15 to 18 minutes or until deep golden-brown. Remove from pans and serve warm, or let cool on racks.

Makes 12 to 16 brioches.

TEXAS STICKY BUNS

3/4 cup warm milk (110F, 45C)
1 (1/4-oz.) pkg. active dry yeast
1/4 cup butter or margarine, cut into small
     pieces, softened
1/4 cup sugar
1 teaspoon salt
2 large eggs
About 3-1/4 cups all-purpose flour

Glaze:
6 tablespoons butter or margarine
1-1/2 tablespoons light corn syrup
1/2 cup packed brown sugar
1/2 cup pecan halves

Filling:
2 tablespoons butter or margarine, melted
     and cooled
1/4 cup packed brown sugar
2 teaspoons ground cinnamon

In a large bowl, combine milk and
yeast; let stand 5 minutes to soften. Add
butter, sugar, salt, 1 whole egg and 1
egg yolk, reserving egg white.

Beat in 3 cups of the flour, 1 cup at a
time, to make a moderately stiff dough.

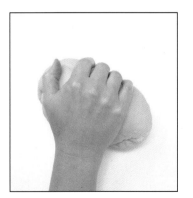

Turn dough onto a floured board and
knead until smooth and satiny, 10 to 20
minutes; add flour as needed to prevent
sticking. Grease a medium-size bowl.
Turn dough over in greased bowl;
cover and let rise in a warm place until
doubled, 1 to 1-1/2 hours.

Knead on floured board to expel air. Let dough rest 10 minutes. Meanwhile, prepare Glaze: In a small pan, cook butter, corn syrup and brown sugar over medium-low heat until sugar dissolves. Immediately pour into a 13" × 9" baking pan; tilt pan so syrup completely covers pan bottom. Arrange pecan halves, flat-side up, on syrup.

Roll out dough into a 18" × 12" rectangle. For the Filling, brush dough with melted butter, then sprinkle with brown sugar and cinnamon. Starting at wide end, roll up jellyroll style. Moisten edge with water and pinch firmly to seal. With a floured sharp knife, cut into 12 slices. Arrange slices, cut-side up, in pan. Cover and let rise in a warm place until doubled in size, about 1 hour.

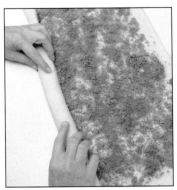

Preheat oven to 350F (175C). In a small bowl, beat reserved egg white beaten with 1 teaspoon water. With a pastry brush, brush rolls with beaten egg white mixture. Bake 30 to 35 minutes or until well browned. Immediately invert onto a serving tray. Serve warm or at room temperature.

Makes 12 rolls.

— NECTARINE-CAJETA TART —

1/3 cup cajeta (Mexican-style caramel sauce)
About 6 ripe, firm nectarines
3 tablespoons pine nuts or slivered almonds
1/3 cup apricot preserves or jam

Pastry:
1 cup all-purpose flour
2 tablespoons sugar
6 tablespoons butter or margarine, chilled
1 large egg

Preheat oven to 350F (175C). Prepare Pastry: In a food processor, process flour, sugar and butter until mixture resembles fine crumbs. Add egg and process until dough holds together.

On a lightly floured surface, roll out Pastry to 1/8 inch thick, and use to line a 10-inch fluted tart pan with removable bottom. Trim edges flush with pan rim. Prick pastry with a fork. Bake 20 minutes or until lightly browned. Let pastry cool before filling.

With a spatula, spread cajeta over crust. Cut nectarines in half and remove seeds. Cut each half into 3/8-inch-wide slices. Overlapping slices slightly, place nectarines on cajeta, starting at the outer edge and working toward the center. Sprinkle nuts over the tart. Bake in a 350F (175C) oven until nectarines are tender, 25 to 30 minutes. In a small pan, heat apricots preserves over low heat until liquid but not bubbly; strain through a sieve. Brush a thick layer over nectarines. Let tart cool.

Makes 10 to 12 servings.

Honey-Glazed Pecan Cake

2/3 cup pecans, toasted
10 tablespoons sugar
1/2 cup butter or margarine, softened
4 large eggs, separated
1 teaspoon vanilla extract
1/3 cup all-purpose flour
1/2 cup honey
2 tablespoons cream sherry
2 tablespoons butter or margarine
3 tablespoons pecans, finely chopped

Preheat oven to 350F (175C). Line a 9-inch round cake pan with waxed paper. Butter and paper flour. In a food processor, process toasted pecans and 2 tablespoons of the sugar into fine crumbs. In a large bowl, beat butter and 5 tablespoons of the sugar until light. Beat in egg yolks, one at a time. Beat in vanilla and pecan mixture until light.

In another bowl, beat egg whites until soft peaks form. Gradually beat in remaining sugar, a tablespoon at a time, until stiff. Fold flour into the butter mixture. Fold in 1/3 of the meringue, then fold in remaining meringue. Spread batter in prepared pan.

Bake 30 to 35 minutes or until cake springs back when lightly touched. Cool on a rack 15 minutes. Turn out of pan and remove paper; turn cake topside up and cool. Prepare glaze: Bring honey, sherry and butter to a boil in a 1-quart pan. Cook over medium-low heat, stirring occasionally, until glaze reaches 235F (110C) on a candy thermometer, about 5 minutes. Spoon glaze over each serving. Decorate with pecans.

Makes 8 servings.

NATILLAS

2 large eggs, separated
1/8 teaspoon cream of tartar
1 whole large egg
8 tablespoons sugar
2 tablespoons all-purpose flour
Pinch of salt
2 cups milk
1 teaspoon vanilla extract
Ground nutmeg

To prepare meringues: Preheat oven to 350F (175C). In a large bowl, beat egg whites with cream of tartar until foamy. Gradually beat in 3 tablespoons of the sugar, 1 tablespoon at a time, until stiff. Fill a 13" × 9" baking pan with about 3/4 inch boiling water. Drop beaten mixture in 8 to 12 equal-size scoops onto water. Bake, uncovered, until golden-brown, 12 to 15 minutes. Lift out meringues with a slotted spoon; place on racks to drain.

In a medium-size bowl, beat egg yolks and whole egg until frothy. Combine remaining sugar, flour and salt. Add to eggs and beat until smooth. In a 2-quart pan, scald milk. Beat hot milk into egg mixture. Return mixture to pan.

Cook, stirring constantly, over medium-low heat until custard thickens, 7 to 9 minutes. Remove from heat and stir in vanilla. Stirring occasionally, let cool. Place meringues in a wide bowl. Pour custard over and around meringues. Sprinkle with nutmeg. Cover and refrigerate 4 to 12 hours.

Makes 4 to 6 servings.

— TEXAS PEACH COBBLER —

6 cups sliced peaches (fresh, frozen or canned)
3/4 cup plus 1 tablespoon sugar
2-1/2 tablespoons cornstarch
1/2 teaspoon each ground cinnamon and
    ground ginger
2 teaspoons lemon juice
1/2 teaspoon vanilla extract
1 tablespoon butter or margarine, quartered
3/4 cup whipping cream

Biscuit Topping:
1 cup all-purpose flour
2 tablespoons sugar
1 teaspoon baking powder
1/4 teaspoon salt
2-1/2 tablespoons butter or margarine, chilled
2-1/2 tablespoons vegetable shortening
1/4 cup finely chopped pecans
1/3 cup milk plus extra for brushing

Preheat oven to 400F (205C). In a large bowl, combine peaches, the 3/4 cup sugar, cornstarch, spices, lemon juice and vanilla. Pour into a shallow 3-quart baking dish. Dot top with butter.

Prepare topping: Sift flour, 1 tablespoon sugar, baking powder and salt into a medium-size bowl. Cut in butter and shortening until mixture resembles coarse crumbs. Stir in pecans and milk until dough leaves side of bowl.

On a floured board, roll out dough to 1/2 inch thick. Using a fluted 2-inch round cutter, cut out circles and place 1 inch apart on top of fruit. Brush with milk; sprinkle with remaining sugar. Bake 35 minutes or until topping is golden-brown. Whip cream with the 1 tablespoon sugar.

Makes 6 to 8 servings.

SOUTHWEST BISCOTTI

1-1/4 cups all-purpose flour
3/4 cup yellow cornmeal
3/4 cup sugar
1 teaspoon baking powder
1/2 teaspoon baking soda
1/2 teaspoon ground cinnamon
1/4 teaspoon ground nutmeg
Dash of salt
2 large eggs, lightly beaten
1/4 cup butter or margarine, melted
1 tablespoon grated orange peel
1 tablespoon plus 1 teaspoon orange juice
1/2 cup pine nuts, toasted

Preheat oven to 350F (175C). Grease a baking sheet. Into a medium-size bowl, sift together flour, cornmeal, sugar, baking powder, soda, spices and salt. In another bowl, combine eggs, butter, orange peel and orange juice. Add egg mixture to dry ingredients and stir until dough holds together and is slightly sticky. Work pine nuts into dough with your hands.

Divide dough into 4 equal portions. On a floured board, roll each portion into a rope about 10 inches long. Place on greased baking sheet and press into a band about 1-1/2 inches wide. Repeat with remaining dough, spacing bands at least 2 inches apart.

Bake 20 minutes or until firm. Cool 5 minutes. With a serrated knife, cut diagonal slices about 1/2 inch thick. Lay the slices flat on the baking sheet and return to a 300F (150C) oven 20 to 25 minutes or until toasted. Let cool, then store in airtight container.

Makes about 60 cookies.

–BLACK & WHITE BISCOCHITOS–

3 cups all-purpose flour
2 teaspoons anise seeds, crushed
1-1/2 teaspoons baking powder
1/4 teaspoon salt
1 cup butter or margarine, softened
2/3 cup sugar
1 large egg
1 tablespoon grated orange peel
1/4 cup brandy
2 tablespoons unsweetened cocoa powder
1/4 cup sugar mixed with 1 teaspoon ground
cinnamon

Preheat oven to 350F (175C). In a medium-size bowl, combine flour, anise seeds, baking powder and salt. In large bowl of an electric mixer, beat butter and the 2/3 cup sugar until fluffy. Beat in egg and orange peel. Gradually add flour mixture alternately with brandy, mixing well after each addition.

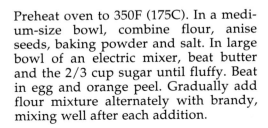

Remove half of dough, gather into a ball and cover with plastic wrap to prevent drying. Sift cocoa into the remaining portion of dough; mix until evenly blended. On a lightly floured surface, roll out chocolate dough to 1/4 inch thick. Cut out cookies with fancy cookie cutters 2 to 2-1/2 inches in diameter. Place slightly apart on ungreased baking sheets. Repeat with white dough.

Lightly sprinkle cinnamon-sugar over all cookies. Bake 10 to 12 minutes or until white cookies are lightly browned and chocolate cookies are firm to the touch. Let cool on wire racks, then store in an airtight container.

Makes about 54 cookies.

Sundaes with Kahlua Sauce

2 (8-inch) flour tortillas
Vegetable oil for deep-frying
1/2 cup powdered sugar, sifted
1 quart vanilla ice cream or coffee ice cream
Whipping cream, whipped
Chocolate-covered coffee beans

Kahlua Sauce:
4 ounces semisweet chocolate, chopped
1/3 cup brewed strong espresso coffee
1 tablespoon honey
2 tablespoons butter, cut into chunks
1/4 cup Kahlua liqueur

With kitchen scissors, cut each tortilla into 6 to 8 wedge-shaped pieces. Heat 2 inches of oil in a 2-quart pan over medium-high heat until oil reaches 360F (180C) on a deep-frying thermometer. Add tortilla pieces, a few at a time, and deep-fry until crisp and lightly browned, 40 to 50 seconds. Remove with a slotted spoon; drain on paper towels.

Place powdered sugar in a small paper bag, add tortillas a few pieces at a time and shake gently to lightly coat with sugar. Let cool.

Prepare sauce: Place chocolate, coffee and honey in a small pan. Cook, stirring constantly, over low heat until chocolate melts. Add butter and stir until melted. Stir in liqueur until mixture is smooth. Use at once, or if you prefer a thicker sauce, refrigerate up to 30 minutes. To assemble sundaes, place 2 scoops of ice cream in each bowl. Top with sauce. Add a dollop of whipped cream, 2 or 3 chocolate-covered coffee beans and sugared tortilla pieces.

Makes 6 servings.

SPICED APPLE SORBET

2/3 cup water
1/2 cup sugar
1 cinnamon stick
1 whole star anise
4 whole allspice berries
3 whole cloves
4 large tart-sweet apples
1-1/4 cups filtered apple juice
2 tablespoons fresh lemon juice
1/4 cup ruby port wine
1 or 2 drops red food coloring (optional)
Fresh mint sprigs and fresh apple slices

Combine water, sugar and spices in a small saucepan. Cover and simmer 20 minutes. Cool and discard spices.

Peel, core and thinly slice apples. Place apples and 1/2 cup of the apple juice into a 2-quart pan. Cover and simmer, stirring occasionally, until apples are very soft, about 20 minutes. Let cool. In a food processor, puree apples and liquid. Add spiced syrup and lemon juice; process until smooth. Divide mixture into 2 equal portions. To half, whisk in 1/2 cup of the apple juice. To the other half, whisk in remaining apple juice, port and food coloring, if used. Pour each portion into an 8- or 9-inch-square pan. Freeze 3 hours or until firm.

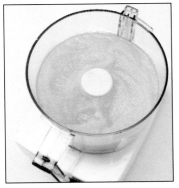

Working with one sorbet, break mixture into small pieces; process in a food processor until slushy. Spoon each sorbet into a 1-quart container. Cover and freeze until firm, about 4 hours or up to 1 week. Scoop into dessert glasses; decorate with mint sprigs and apple slices.

Makes 6 servings (1 quart sorbet).

— ALMOND COOKIE TACOS —

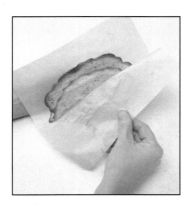

1/2 cup sliced almonds
2 tablespoons all-purpose flour
2 tablespoons sugar
2 large egg whites
1 tablespoon butter or margarine, melted
2 to 2-1/2 cups berries or diced fruit
2 teaspoons fresh lemon juice
1 tablespoon sugar or to taste

Preheat oven to 350F (175C). Cut 4 (8-inch) squares of parchment or waxed paper. In a food processor, process 1/3 cup almonds, flour and sugar until nuts are finely chopped. Add remaining nuts; process until nuts are coarsely chopped. Add egg whites and butter; process briefly to mix.

For each cookie, place about 2-1/2 tablespoons of the batter on a sheet of parchment; thinly spread to make a 5-inch circle. Slide 2 cookies onto a baking sheet. Bake 10 to 12 minutes or until edges of cookies are golden-brown and centers are light-brown. If one cookie browns before the second one, lift it from pan and shape.

To shape each cookie, fold parchment so cookie resembles a taco. Gently pull off parchment and turn cookie upside down into a small bowl so it will hold its shape while it cools. Work quickly; if cookies cool, they cannot be bent without breaking. Bake and shape the other 2 cookies. Just before serving, combine berries and fruits. Stir in lemon juice and sugar. To serve, place a cookie on each of 4 dessert plates. Fill cookies with fruit.

Makes 4 servings.

Canyon Road Spiced Cider

2 quarts cider or filtered apple juice
1/3 cup firmly packed brown sugar
8 whole allspice berries
8 whole cloves
3 cinnamon sticks
2 thin slices gingerroot
1 orange
2 tablespoons raisins

Pour cider into a 3- to 4-quart non-reactive pan; stir in brown sugar.

Place allspice, cloves, cinnamon sticks and ginger root into a 12-inch square of cheesecloth. Bring corners together and tie; drop spice bag into cider. Bring to a simmer. Cover and simmer 20 minutes. Discard spice bag.

Cut orange in half lengthwise, then cut crosswise to make 1/8-inch-thick half slices (discard ends). On bamboo skewers, thread lengthwise 1 orange slice; skewer 4 or 5 raisins below orange slice. Ladle hot cider into mugs or cups and place a skewer of fruit in each.

Makes 8 servings.

NEW MEXICAN HOT CHOCOLATE

1/4 cup unsweetened cocoa powder
1/4 cup sugar
1/2 teaspoon ground cinnamon
Dash of salt
1/2 cup water
3-1/2 cups milk
1 teaspoon vanilla extract
1/2 teaspoon almond extract
4 cinnamon sticks (optional)

In a 2-quart pan, combine cocoa, sugar, ground cinnamon, salt and water. Cook, stirring, over medium heat until mixture is smooth.

Add milk and bring to a simmer. Add vanilla and almond extract.

With a portable electric mixer or rotary beater, whip hot chocolate until foamy. Pour into mugs. Place a cinnamon stick in each mug, if desired.

Makes 4 servings.

CAFE MEXICANO

1 small cone piloncillo (Mexican raw sugar)
  or 2 tablespoons firmly packed dark
  brown sugar
1/4 cup coffee-flavored liqueur
2 tablespoons brandy
4 cups hot brewed coffee
Whipped cream

Crush piloncillo.

Stir 1 tablespoon of piloncillo or brown sugar, coffee-flavored liqueur and brandy into hot coffee. Let stand 1 minute, stirring, until sugar dissolves.

Pour into 4 heatproof mugs or glasses. Garnish each serving with a dollop of whipped cream. Sprinkle a generous pinch of piloncillo or brown sugar over each serving, if desired.

Makes 4 servings.

MARGARITAS

Coarse salt
1 lime, cut into wedges
1 (6-oz.) can frozen limeade concentrate
3/4 cup tequila
1/4 cup Triple Sec
3 to 4 cups ice cubes
Lime twists, to decorate
Lime peel, to decorate

Pour about 1/2 inch salt into a shallow bowl. Rub rims of 6 cocktail glasses with lime wedges; stand glasses, rim-side down, in salt to coat the rims.

In a blender, combine frozen lime concentrate, tequila, Triple Sec and ice cubes. Blend until ice is finely chopped and mixture is slushy.

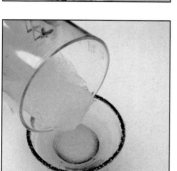

Pour into glasses, taking care that liquid does not drip onto the salt rims. Decorate as desired.

Makes 6 servings.

Variation
Margaritas on the Rocks: *Prepare recipe above but do not process in blender with ice. Instead, combine Margarita mixture with 1-1/2 cups chilled club soda. Place 3 or 4 ice cubes in each glass; pour drinks over ice in each glass. Garnish as desired.*

METRIC CHART

Comparison to Metric Measure				
When You Know	**Symbol**	**Multiply By**	**To Find**	**Symbol**
teaspoons	tsp	5.0	milliliters	ml
tablespoons	tbsp	15.0	milliliters	ml
fluid ounces	fl. oz.	30.0	milliliters	ml
cups	c	0.24	liters	l
pints	pt.	0.47	liters	l
quarts	qt.	0.95	liters	l
ounces	oz.	28.0	grams	g
pounds	lb.	0.45	kilograms	kg
Fahrenheit	F	5/9 (after subtracting 32)	Celsius	C

Fahrenheit to Celsius	
F	**C**
200—205	95
220—225	105
245—250	120
275	135
300—305	150
325—330	165
345—350	175
370—375	190
400—405	205
425—430	220
445—450	230
470—475	245
500	260

Liquid Measure to Milliliters		
1/4 teaspoon	=	1.25 milliliters
1/2 teaspoon	=	2.5 milliliters
3/4 teaspoon	=	3.75 milliliters
1 teaspoon	=	5.0 milliliters
1-1/4 teaspoons	=	6.25 milliliters
1-1/2 teaspoons	=	7.5 milliliters
1-3/4 teaspoons	=	8.75 milliliters
2 teaspoons	=	10.0 milliliters
1 tablespoon	=	15.0 milliliters
2 tablespoons	=	30.0 milliliters

Liquid Measure to Liters		
1/4 cup	=	0.06 liters
1/2 cup	=	0.12 liters
3/4 cup	=	0.18 liters
1 cup	=	0.24 liters
1-1/4 cups	=	0.3 liters
1-1/2 cups	=	0.36 liters
2 cups	=	0.48 liters
2-1/2 cups	=	0.6 liters
3 cups	=	0.72 liters
3-1/2 cups	=	0.84 liters
4 cups	=	0.96 liters
4-1/2 cups	=	1.08 liters
5 cups	=	1.2 liters
5-1/2 cups	=	1.32 liters

INDEX